D1682766

THE CANARY ISLANDS
THROUGH HISTORY

SALVADOR LOPEZ HERRERA
PROFESSOR AT THE MADRID UNIVERSITY

THE CANARY ISLANDS THROUGH HISTORY

FOREWORD
BY
MANUEL BALLESTEROS
GAIBROIS

editorial dosbe
Avda. Menéndez Pelayo, 83

MADRID
1978

Traslated from the Spanish original
«Las Islas Canarias a través de la Historia»
(3rd. edition)
by
VERONICA DE LA TORRE
Lecturer in English Language
at Madrid University

© **SALVADOR LOPEZ HERRERA**
Printed in Spain; MADRID, 1978

I.S.B.N.: 84-400-4706-1
Depósito legal: M-11.314-1978

SERVICIOS EDITORIALES GRÁFICOS; Menéndez Pelayo, 83. Madrid-7

FOREWORD

FOREWORD

When writing the foreword to a book, one often tends to either speak about the work itself or try to introduce its author to the prospective reader. In this short preface, however, both the author and the book will be dealt with.

Many years ago —around 1940— Professor Antonio Ballesteros Beretta appointed as his assistant professor a young man from the Island of La Palma in the Canary Islands. Salvador López Herrera was then fresh from the university and about to begin his Doctoral Dissertation on a subject closely related to the Canary Islands and America: the biography of Father Jose the Anchieta, the heroic son of La Laguna who founded San Pablo de Piratininga. That young lecturer, Salvador López Herrera, is now a Doctor in History, a university professor, and the author of a good number of works. His career during these years has been that of a devoted lover of learning —crystallized in lectures, articles, books, and dissertations in international council meetings, like the one held in Sao Paulo in 1954, the occasion of which was the centennary of the foundation of the city by the Jesuit whose biography López Herrera had written.

His major contribution to historical studies has been in the field of the relationship between the Canaries and America, tracing the progress of illustrious sons of the islands and their descendants in those lands beyond the seas. A reliable historian and a true specialist in the subject —as the reader will see— Salvador López Herrera embellishes History with literary lyricism, coupling this beauty of style with sound scientific research and commendable critical judgement.

And what about the book itself? In its pages the reader will find a vast historical survey: the origins and development of human culture from the dawn of History up to the establishment of European culture in the archipelago of the Hesperides, the Fortunate Islands, the Islands of Dogs or the Canaries. Also reviewed in the impeccable pages of the book are theories about Atlantis —a controversial subject on which the author avoids taking sides— the process of its population, the secular customs of the Old Guanches, their spiritual and physical culture, and the dramatic arrival of the Europeans: Bretons, Galicians, and Andalusians under the Sire de Bethencourt...

The book contains a remarkably happy historical synthesis, where the reader is easily led from geography to ethnography and then to history, without forgetting a relevant anecdote or a touch of lyricism in quotations from writers who were interested in the Canaries or visited them. From the whistled language of La Gomera and the petroglyphs of Belmaco —following the chronological rigour that is History's due— we come to the important part played by the Canaries in America and in the European process of colonization. And this is what is particularly relevant to the Canaries: the fact that the Europeans (whether Spanish, Portuguese, or Breton) lent them their culture and their modern civilization without the usual bloodbath or the extermination of the first settlers of the islands, who mixed with the newcomers and whose imprint is still alive and easily perceptible.

There is only one thing more I would want to say, and this I am glad to do with full confidence: the book you have now in your hands is one well worth reading.

MANUEL BALLESTEROS GAIBROIS,
Professor of American History at
Madrid University.

TABLE OF CONTENTS

	Page
INTRODUCTION	21

CHAPTER I

GEOGRAPHICAL CHARACTERISTICS OF THE CANARY ISLANDS	23
1.—Geographical Description	25
2.—The Best Climate in the World	26
3.—Crops Found in all Climates	27
4.—Typical Vegetation, Peculiar Only to the Canary Islands	27
5.—The Canarian Landscape	28
6.—Geological Formation	31

CHAPTER II

GENESIS OF THE CANARY ISLANDS	35
Atlantis	37

CHAPTER III

PREHISTORIC TIMES	53
1.—Legendary Times	55
2.—The Origin of the Name of the Canary Islands	57
3.—Phoenician, Carthaginian, and Roman Expeditions	58
4.—Origin of the Gaunches, their Physical Characteristics and their Mingling with the other Races	60
5.—Analogies Between the Gaunches and the Cro-Magnon Race.	63
6.—Spreading of the Cro-Magnon Race over Europe and its Settlement in the Canary Islands	63
7.—Persistence of the Gaunche Type in the Present Population of the Canary Islands	64

CHAPTER IV

CANARIAN CIVILIZATION IN PRE-CONQUEST DAYS ... 69

1.—Language ... 71
2.—Food ... 71
3.—Dress ... 72
4.—Social Hierarchy ... 72
5.—Industry ... 73
6.—Marriage ... 74
7.—Religion ... 74
8.—Public Holidays and Festivals ... 75
9.—Weapons ... 76
10.—The Mencey's Coronation ... 76
11.—Housing ... 77
12.—Mummification ... 77
13.—Law ... 78
14.—A Whistled Language ... 78

CHAPTER V

CAVE INSCRIPTIONS IN THE CANARY ISLANDS AND POSSIBLE ANALOGIES WITH OTHER INSCRIPTIONS IN THE AMERICAN CONTINENT ... 81

1.—Rock Carvings ... 83
2.—Evidence Pointing to Early Contacts Between the Primitive Inhabitants of the Canary Island and Those of the American Continent ... 87

CHAPTER VI

A PRELUDE TO THE CONQUEST OF THE ARCHIPELAGO ... 91

1.—Expeditions which Preceded the Conquest of the Canary Islands ... 93
2.—Don Luis de la Cerda, Príncipe de la Fortuna ... 97
3.—Other Expeditions to the Archipelago ... 98

CHAPTER VII

THE CONQUEST OF THE CANARIES UNDER THE PATRONAGE OF THE CROWN OF CASTILE ... 101

1.—Aspects of the Conquest ... 103
2.—A Warlike Race ... 104
3.—Juan de Bethencourt, First Conqueror of the Canaries ... 104

4.—Brief Account of Bethencourt's Expedition to Lanzarote and Fuerteventura   106
 5.—Bethencourt Pays Homage to the King of Castile in the Name of the Canary Islands   107
 6.—Berthin de Berneval's Rebellion   108
 7.—Atchen's Treason. The Outbreak of War   109
 8.—Gadifer's Visit to the Canarian Archipelago   109
 9.—Bethencourt's Return and the Surrender of Lanzarote   110
10.—Second Expedition to Fuerteventura and Account of Some of the Events Which Took Place There   110
11.—Dangerous Disagreements Between the Two Commanders of the Expedition   111
12.—Fuerteventura's Surrender   112
13.—Bethencourt's Third Voyage to Europe   112
14.—Bethencourt's Return to the Canary Islands   113
15.—Bethencourt's Visit to the African Coast and the Canarian Archipelago   114
16.—The Conquest of the Island of Hierro   115
17.—Bethencourt's Return to his Native Country   117
18.—Death of Bethencourt   119

CHAPTER VIII

SUBSEQUENT PROTECTIVE POLICY OF THE KINGS OF CASTILE IN THE CONQUEST OF THE CANARY ISLANDS   121

1.—Maciot de Bethencourt's Administration and Subsequent Cession of the Canary Islands   123
2.—Various Transactions and Cessions Involving the Canary Islands   124
3.—Occupation of Gomera and Attempts at Invading the Other Islands   125
4.—Diego de Herrera's Enterprise   127
5.—Political Organization of the Islands of Tenerife, Gran Canaria, and La Palma in Pre-Conquest Days   130

CHAPTER IX

THE CATHOLIC MONARCHS UNDERTAKE THE CONQUEST OF THE ISLANDS OF GRAN CANARIA, TENERIFE, AND LA PALMA   135

A.—THE CONQUEST OF GRAN CANARIA

1.—Juan Rejón's Expedition   137
2.—The Battle of Guiniguada   138

		Page
3.—Dissensions between Rejón and Dean Bermúdez		139
4.—The Attack on Tirajana		140
5.—Juan Rejón Returns to the Canaries		140
6.—Juan Rejón Is Discharged and Replaced by Pedro de Vera.		141
7.—Pedro de Vera's First Political Moves		141
8.—The Death of Doramas		142
9.—The Agaete Fortress is Built. Second Battle of Tirajana ...		143
10.—Return and Death of Juan Rejón		143
11.—The Attack on Galdar. Subjection of its Guanarteme		144
12.—Further Exploits Performed by Pedro de Vera		145
13.—Gran Canaria Is Conquered At Last		145
14.—Uprisings in Gomera and Death of Hernán Peraza, Son of Diego de Herrera		147

CHAPTER X

B.—Conquest of La Palma and Tenerife   149

1.—Alonso Fernández de Lugo is Appointed Captain-General of the Unconquered Islands	151
2.—First Tactical Moves in La Palma	152
3.—Attack on the Caldera and the Island's Surrender	153
4.—The Landing at Tenerife. Early Clashes	155
5.—The Guanche Princes League Together	156
6.—The Battle of Acentejo	157
7.—The Attack on the Tower of the Encampment. Retreat to Gran Canaria	158
8.—A Further Expedition Against the Guanches. Battle of La Laguna	159
9.—Further Progress of the Conquering Army. Plague Decimates the Guanches	161
10.—The Feat of the Twelve Soldiers	161
11.—Food Shortage at the Spanish Camp. Lope Hernández de la Guerra's generous Gesture	162
12.—The Second Battle of Acentejo	163
13.—The Spaniards Invade the Valley of Arautapola and Tenerife is Finally Conquered	164

CHAPTER XI

The Colonization of the Islands; Contribution of the Canaries to the Conquest and Colonization of America   169

A.—Colonization of the Canary Islands Under the Patronage of the Spanish Monarchs	171
B.—Canarian Contribution to the Conquest and Colonization of America	173

	Page
APPENDICES	
I.—Atlantis in Pato's Works	181
II.—The Tiahuanaco Ruins	187
SELECTED BIBLIOGRAPHY	193

LIST OF ILLUSTRATIONS

	Page
I.—Blooming Tajinastes, at the foot of the Teide	24-25
II.—Tree of Stone with the Teide in the background ...	24-25
III.—The age-old Dragon-tree at Icod de los Vinos, Tenerife	24-25
IV.—Sanctuary of Our Lady of the Snow, surrounded by «pinus canariensis» in Santa Cruz de la Palma	24-25
V.—Location of Atlantis, according to Plato's Description.	40-41
VI.—Contour of the Atlantic Ocean, and of the submerged portion of the ancient island of Atlantis, according to Donnelly	40-41
VII.—Upper section of the huge portico of Tiahuanaco ruins, where the mythical figure and the calendar are carved	40-41
VIII.—Stone heads discovered at the Tiahuanaco ruins ...	40-41
IX.—Mummified Guanche heads, taken from various burial caves	65-66
X.—Necklaces worn by the Guanches. They were made from terra-cotta beads and sea-shells	65-66
XI.—Typical Garafía costumes, Island of La Palma	72-73
XII.—Banana trees and girls dressed in the typical Tazacorte costume, Island of La Palma	72-73
XIII.—The National Park at the Caldera de Taburiente, Island of La Palma	72-73
XIV.—The snow-covered peak of the Teide	72-73
XV.—Whistled language, typical among the natives, Island of Gomera	80-81

		Page
XVI.	Traditional Chipude pottery, made by the women with extraordinary artistry, Island of Gomera	80-81
XVII.	The Schaman drum, according to Hermann Wirth in: **Die Heilige Urschheit**	88-89
XVIII.	Signs assembled in a way which suggest they may from words, found in the inscriptions in Hierro	88-89
XIX.	Petroglyphs carved on the rocks, at the entrance to the Belmaco cave, La Palma, Canary Island	88-89
XX.	Inscriptions from the Candía ravine (Hierro). Canary Islands	88-89
XXI.	The prehistoric cave of Belmaco, at Mazo, Island of La Palma, with rock carvings	104-105
XXII.	Prehistoric cave of la Zarza, Garafía, Island of La Palma, with rock carvings	104-105
XXIII.	Juan de Bethencourt, first conqueror of the Canaries.	104-105
XXIV.	The Conquest's Cross, at the parish church of La Concepción, Santa Cruz de Tenerife	104-105
XXV.	The Orotava Valley, Tenerife	120-121
XXVI.	Partial View of the Realejo coast, Tenerife	120-121
XXVII.	Arucas, Gran Canaria	120-121
XXVIII.	Santa Cruz de la Palma seen from the «Risco de la Concepción»	120-121
XXIX.	Parish church of El Salvador, an architectural masterpiece from the sixteenth century, Santa Cruz de la Palma	136-137
XXX.	Los Tilos, at San Andrés y Sauces, Island of La Palma.	136-137
XXXI.	The caves of Las Cruces and the hermitage of Valerón, historical remains of the Guanche «habitat», Las Palmas	136-137
XXXII.	The Tejeda Valley and Roque Nublo in Gran Canaria.	136-137
XXXIII.	Panoramic view of San Andrés y Sauces, Island of La Palma	152-153
XXXIV.	The Blue Lagoon, in San Andrés y Sauces, Island of La Palma	152-153

		Page
XXXV.	Partial view of the coastline and the Lighthouse of Barlovento, Island of La Palma	152-153
XXXVI.	Partial view of Fuencaliente, Island of La Palma ...	152-153
XXXVII.	A typical scene, with the Montaña del Fuego (Fire Mountain) in the background, Lanzarote	168-169
XXXVIII.	The Infierno de Timanfaya, inside this mound temperature rises above 400 ºC., Lanzarote	168-169
XXXIX.	Panoramic view of Puerto Rosario, capital of Fuerteventura	168-169
XL.	Montaña del Fuego (Fire Mountain). Lanzarote ...	168-169
XLI.	The House of the Colonels, with rich baroque decorations. Fuerteventura	184-185
XLII.	Slag and lava land which the native peasants turn into fertile orchards. Lanzarote	184-185
XLIII.	Plato. Marble bust (Vatican Museum)	184-185
XLIV.	Monolith called «El Fraile» (The Friar), at the Tiahuanaco ruins	184-185

MAPS

I.—Map of the Canary Islands, drawn up in the year 1686 by Pedro Agustín del Castillo-León Ruiz de Vergara (page 4 of the cover).

II.—The Canary Islands in modern times 196-197

INTRODUCTION

The Canary Islands, just a few dots in the expanse of the Atlantic Ocean, seem to have a providential task to fulfill in the history of Western Civilization. Their names had a legendary splendour in classical times, a poetic aura surrounded them in the Middle Ages —with the fascinating descriptions of the islands of the Seven Cities, St. Brandan, and Brazil— and they win a preeminent place in modern times as the advance post en route to those lands beyond the sea, having offered Christopher Columbus their hospitaly on the eve of, perhaps, the greatest event in modern History.

We would need too many pages to describe in detail the Canary Islands: their geographical situation, their geological formation, their historical evolution, and their climate, vegetation and landscape. These islands, graced by God with an incomparable beauty, light and colour, and sights of breathtaking splendour are all of interest to the reader who wants to visit or at least experience vicariously through his imagination these marvels.

Classical historians painted the Canaries as a privileged land, and there placed the Elysium, the Garden of Hesperides that mysterious region which they clothed in the most poetical of legends. Many of them believed the Canaries to be the remains of the unknown and lost Atlantis. Herodotus situated there the confines of the world, where the sea could no longer be sailed; where the Hesperides were; and where Mount Atlas, with its conical peak, bore the weight of the heavens. Juba, King of Mauritania, regarded the Fortunate Islands as the land where the sun never set —night was to be created by the Hesperides to protect their golden apples.

Adorned by beauty and mystery in constant juxtaposition, the Canaries have attracted the most famous modern poets who have obtained there the source of inspiration for their immortal works.

Perhaps one of the most peculiar features in the islands is the transitional character they possess. From among the various lands moulded by Castile into one nation, the Canaries were the least influenced. Their geographical position places them strategically as an outpost of Europe, a sentinel of Africa and an antechamber of America.

CHAPTER I

Geographical Characteristics of The Canary Islands

1.1.—Geographical Description

1.2.—The Best Climate in the World

1.3.—Crops Found in all Climates

1.4.—Typical Vegetation, Peculiar Only to the Canary Islands

1.5.—The Canarian Landscape

1.6.—Geological Formation

1.—Blooming Tajinastes, at the foot of the Teide.

II.—Tree of Stone with the Teide in the background.

III.—The age-old Dragon-tree at Icod de los Vinos, Tenerife.

IV.—Sanctuary of Our Lady of the Snow, surrounded by «pinus canariensis» in Santa Cruz de la Palma.

1.—GEOGRAPHICAL DESCRIPTION

Few lands may boast of such an interesting landscape as the Canaries. These islands in the Atlantic possess more than enough natural beauties to captivate those who visit them, and even to astound those with a higher sensibility.

The traveller is enchanted by the depth of their valleys, the grandiosity of their mountains, and the profuseness of their vegetation —in dramatic contrast to the barren landscape of the neighbouring Sahara desert.

The Canary Islands are situated 115 kilometers from the coasts of Mauritania Tingitana and 705 miles from Cadiz. In them one finds the last Spanish port on the way to America and the first upon returning to Spain. The archipelago is formed by 7 major islands and 6 minor ones, which cover a total land area of 7,666 kilometers —7,573 kilometers comprise the inhabited islands and 93 kilometers the uninhabited ones. The archipelago is divided into 2 provinces: Tenerife and Las Palmas. Tenerife, Palma, Gomera, and Hierro belong to the former while Canaria; Lanzarote and Fuerteventura belong to the latter.

The poetry that emanates from these islands so inspired the classical world that they were endowed with the dream-like quality of a legend, their profiles blurred in the twilight of prehistory.

Later on the Canaries, because of their strategic position, experienced capital events in modern history. Thus they saw Christopher Columbus venturing across an unknown sea to offer new glory to the Crown of Castile; Nelson, who lost his arm in St. Cruz de Tenerife and there knew the bitterness of defeat; and Napoleon who, on his way to exile and death, saw his bright star disappear one silver evening behind the gigantic mass of the Teide.

2.—The Best Climate in the World

The climate is so mild that in classical times the islands were called the Elysium, the land of the blessed, the Fortunate Islands. The Canaries have an exceptionally good weather throughout the 4 seasons, without brusque changes from one season to another. Their geographical situation, their soil, and their vegetation all contribute to this very special privilege. The average temperature never rises above 25 ºC in the summer nor descends below 12 ºC in the winter.

Situated amidst the Gulf Stream and protected by the trade winds, the Canary Islands have, in truth, no winter. Because of its southern position, the Archipelago hardly ever suffers from low temperatures. Days are always warm and sunny —never excessively hot as it is cooled by winds from the northeast while the winter is mild and bound to no variations.

The Canaries enjoy a climate unrivalled throughout the world; statistics have shown that there are no more than 69 rainy days per year and at night there is no dampness, not even at sunrise or at sunset. This mildness and temperateness allows even the ailing to sleep with their windows open.

Coupled with this exceptional climate is the warm and friendly temper of the islanders who, in spite of their frequent contact with other European countries and America, have proudly kept their deeply rooted Spanish tradition. The women from the Canaries, famed for their beauty and feminine charm, sum up in themselves the eternal smile of this land and the purity of its sky. And as the folk song says, the rhythmic «folía»:

> All the women from the islands
> Resemble the gigantic Teide
> Snow shows in their faces
> But fire burns in their hearts

3.—Crops Found in all Climates

Another of the privileges the islands enjoy is the readiness of their soil and climate to grow the American pineapple and the tropical banana side by side with the cherry and apple tree. Because of this unique feature, one could probably surmise that the whole of the Earth's vegetation may be found there. The camellias are 10 meters high, bursting into 10,000 flowers. A variety of trees thrive there: mangos, papayas, avocados, almonds, camphor, and all kinds of palm trees to name a few.

4.—Typical Vegetation, Peculiar Only to the Canary Islands

The laurel species (Canarian laurel tree, *laurus canariensis;* barbuzano, *apollonia canariensis;* Viñátigo, *pérsea indica;* etc.) flower in all their beauty in these islands. Sad to say, they have practically disappeared in other regions of the globe.

The Canarian pine tree, *pinus canariensis,* and the dragon tree, *dracaena draco,* are two typical species and splendid specimens of these may be found in almost every island. The dragon-tree has an enormously long life; when an incision is made, a red fluid called «dragon's blood» oozes from the tree and turns into reddish powder when dried. Two of the most beautiful dragon-trees in the Canaries can be seen in La Laguna and in Icod.

«The dragon-tree is a tree native to the East, a species of which is found only in the Canary Islands. Under the broad canopy of its branches the "guanche" kings listened to plaintiffs and the "maga" princesses danced, those same princesses that the conquerors saw washing clothes in the rivulets.

One of the most beautiful is found in Icod. They are giants, titans that take centuries to grow. They may be called the elephants of the vegetable kingdom. All their branches grow downwards, to sink into the ground and turn into roots; they have to be cut to prevent them from covering the tree altogether. The leaves resemble clusters of steely daggers and the sap, red and bright, is known as "dragon's blood".»

5.—THE CANARIAN LANDSCAPE

«... (These were) the Elysian Fields which are in the confines of the world, where men lead peaceful lives, without suffering from snow, hard winters or rain, enjoying an air perennially cool, a product of breezes from the ocean.»

(HOMER, *The Odyssey*, Book IV)

In all probability, Homer may have been referring to the Canaries. The great Roman poets also thought the Canaries a sort of fairyland; and thus Horace encourages the Romans to flee from civil war and cross the ocean in search of those prosperous islands:

«There the soil offers bread, without the discomforts of ploughing, and also all kinds of fruit... Jupiter set these islands apart from the rest of the world, so that they would become a shelter for virtuous men. There you will suffer neither from heat nor from cold and vermin and poisonous reptiles are unknown to this privileged land.»

(HORACE, *Ode 16*, Book V)

Virgil depicts the Fortunate Islands in his characteristic, luminous style:

«Aeneas and the Sybil —he says— arrived at last to the lovely places, the peaceful gardens in the fortunate woods, the fortunate islands, where the happy spirits dwell. Their sky is purer and brighter than ours, so that the fields are bathed in a purple light. The fortunate ones know them and are able to locate their stars, because they are clearer and more resplendent than the rest.»

(VIRGIL, *Aeneid*, Book VI)

But there is one picture of the Canaries that far surpasses the praises written by the classical poets. Enraptured by the Island's beauty, Luciano writes:

«Spring dwells forever in the fields of the Fortunate Islands, and only the pleasant zephyr blows there. And in truth, that land is always green and flowers grow in thick clusters, and plants are neither coarse nor dark. Vineyards yield their fruits twice a year and offer every month the plentiful tithe of their grapes. I have heard that pomegranate trees, and apple trees give thirteen crops every year. For they said that in the month called Minons in those islands, trees bear fruit twice.

Moreover, corn ears, instead of producing grain, yield perfectly finished loaves of bread, which grow almost like fungii. They have many fountains in their city. Of these, three hundred and seventy five pour water, an equal amount pour honey and there are five hundred which pour oil, balm, and diverse aromatic liquours. And these fountains are nothing if compared to the seven rivers of milk and eight of wine. Parties are held outside the town, in the field called Elysium, a lovely place surrounded by a wood in which all kinds of trees grow, which spread their shade over those lying on the ground. Meat is made from flowers. The winds bring whatever delicacies are desired; the only thing they do not provide is wine, but the guests have no need for it, as nearby there are some huge diaphanous trees, which are made of glistening glass, and bear fruits in the shape of lovely cups, as beautiful in their proportions as in the artistry with which they are made.

So, upon arriving to the place where the party is held, the guests pick one or two of these cups and no sooner are they laid on the table that they fill with wine.

Nightingales and other songbirds serve as crowns or garlands in the gathering. And other birds, bearing in their beaks flowers from the neighbouring fields, flutter over the heads of the guests, thus blending together their song and their flight.

Perfume is provided in this way: thick clouds suck aromatic liquours from fountains and rivers, then they hover over the festive gathering and by and by the winds make them exude rare, exquisite liquours which resemble dew.»

(LUCIANO, *De Verae Historiae*)

Humboldt, the famous naturalist, also wrote about these islands. When speaking about the Orotava Valley in Tenerife, he commented:

«When entering the Orotava Valley, one discovers a fascinating land which has enchanted travellers from all over the world.

In my visits to tropical lands, I have encountered places where nature is more majestic and richer in its growth; but after the banks of the Orinoco, the mountain ranges of Peru and the lovely Mexican valleys, I must admit that I have never seen a picture as variegated, harmonious and attractive as that offered in the Orotava Valley by the striking contrast between the greenery of vegetation and the masses of rock.

I can only compare this sight to the bays of Genoa and Naples, but the Orotava far exceeds these by the size of its masses of rock and the luxuriance of its vegetation.

Mr. Anderson, the naturalist who took part in Captain Cook's third voyage, advised European physicians to send their patients to Tenerife.

However, it is rather difficult to offer an accurate description of the Canarian landscape. It is necessary to visit this privileged land in order to admire sights unique in the world.

When touring any of these islands, we are offered a new landscape with every turn of the road; from the Egyptian decor to the lush postcard from the West Indies; from the rugged northern landscape to the soft plains where sugar cane and palm trees grow.

The island of La Palma is endowed with many places worth visiting. Here is the biggest crater in the world which the islanders call "Caldera de Taburiente". It is an old, monogenous, extinct volcano, about 28,000 meters in circumference, 9,000 in diameter, and 707 in depth. It has an enormous interest, both scientific and as an impressive landscape feature. It offers the traveller the most dramatic sights: waterfalls capering down the rocks, bottomless pits, and fantastic vegetation —from gigantic ferns to old, huge pine trees in a ghostly descent down its slopes. No less interesting are the birds and wild beasts seen there and "Idafe" the sacred monolith, the altar used by the natives in primitive times to worship the god Abora, which still stands as a sylvan symbol of an ancestral cult. And all this is surrounded by a vast ampitheatre of steep peaks, which is often covered with snow. This huge and unique volcano may be seen from all the higher mountains in the island, offering the visitor the grandiose sight of the biggest crater on earth. The rocks, rising from the sea depths, cover the two kilometers of its steep slope, rushing past that garland of white clouds and fulfilling God's work in building the most beautiful minaret one could dream: with the Caldera on one side, the island's silhouette is clearly cut in its totality, the sea foam tracing arabesques and the Atlantic waters, as if born below these rocks, spread towards the horizon where the neighbouring islands rise. The Teide emerges in the distance, that immense mountain which, according to a folk song, was cast in the Caldera's crucible. All harmonies and all hues crystallized in this island and nothing else was needed, because, conjured by light, land, water and fire, and lacking no lesser beauty in the most beautiful sight imaginable, a triumphant music was heard...»

6.—GEOLOGICAL FORMATION

There are various theories about the geological formation of these islands. Some geologists maintain that they emerged from the sea as a result of the activity of submarine volcanoes; others assert that they are the remains of a lost continent, Atlantis. Some historians, Cronau among them, belive that this was an enormous continent, stretching from the western coasts of Europe to those of America. And thus, the name «Antilles» is a corruption of «Atlantis». No matter which of these hypotheses one believes in, its authenticity is still a matter of speculation.

Doubtless, there are several data which point to the Canarian archipelago as being of purely volcanic origin, unconnected to the modern changes in the Western coasts of Morocco. According to Lyell, the Canaries were a product of volcanic activity and *they were never joined to the continent*. This view is shared by Fischer, de Pallary, Reclus, Bomgigner, Oswald, Heer and nearly all the geologists, like Martung, who have studied the Archipelago.

The opposite theory —that the Canaries are a part of the lost continent of Atlantis— was advanced by Forbes and maintained by Unger, Bory de Saint-Vincent, and Termier. This theory was born from the need to justify the obvious affinities to the European, African, and American flora and fauna in the Tertiary period, and the similitude between the Canarian coasts and those of the nearest American, African and European coastal areas.

Atlantis, that very controversial matter, is intimately linked to the geological formation of the Canaries. Many scholars believe that the archipelago is what remained after the cataclysmic destruction of Atlantis.

Gaffarel thinks that the Antilles, the Canaries, and the Azores are the vertices of an immense, triangular island which, well after the Tertiary period, sank under the ocean because of land movements, leaving these islands as mute witnesses of its one-time existence. Tenerife's smoky peak is said to be a symbol of the terrible volcanic convulsion that was part of the whole tremendous cataclysm. Thus, this may explain how the Americans found a passage to Africa and Spain. (Chapter V of this book will review this further.)

One of the characters in Benoit's *Atlantis* said, when within the sight of the Algerian coasts: «I am sorry for those who, on first seeing these softly coloured rocks, don't feel their hearts leap on thinking that this land did once stretch for thousands and thousands of miles...»

The academician Saavedra, also maintains that:

«Far beyond the pillars of Hercules, there was an island as big as a continent, where a nation, the Atlantes, lived. Its ten kings, forming a coalition, conquered part of Europe and the whole of Lybia and were in the end vanquished in a formidable struggle by the first Athenians. These Atlantes lived reaching a high degree of civilization, ruled over various neighbouring islands, and travelled by sea to other continents beyond their island. Their laws and customs were a good example of political organization and social balance; but towards the end of their domination, they sank into piteous corruption and the enraged gods punished them by a terrible cataclysm which condemned Atlantis to the fathomless sea depths, which from then onwards were covered in such a thick mire that it was impossible to sail those waters again. In classical times, geographers accepted beyond doubt the one-time existence of this island and its subsequent disappearance; but Neoplatonists found cause to doubt this theory, and afterwards denied any historical truth to this account. It was only later on, when America was discovered and geological and hydrographical researches were intensified, that the question was raised once again. We hear new hypotheses nearly every day, which try to give a scientific and historical explanation to Plato's theory, and account for a possible contact through land with the American natives.

The eminent historian, Professor Antonio Ballesteros Beretta, when writing about Plato's famous Atlantis said:

«For many centuries, men have worshipped this jewel which was avidly read during the Middle Ages, in the Latin translation made by Calcidius in the sixth century A. D. The style is far from clear, which contributes to making it one of the most abstruse books in classical antiquity. But this very obscurity lends it a mysterious fascination. The main theme is the formation of the world's soul and all that pertains man...»

CHAPTER II

Genesis of The Canary Islands

ATLANTIS

ATLANTIS

Viera y Clavijo, perhaps the greatest among the historians who have devoted their attention to the Canaries, says that these islands are no mere eruptions of volcanos though fire, as in a chemical laboratory, played a hand in shaping most of the primitive land. He also adds:

«Was this ocean called the Atlantic because it stands where Plato's famous Atlantis stood before its destruction? Or were these islands called Atlantic because they are the remains, the reliques, the higher peaks of that unhappy land? I would not dare to put these questions forth if Plato's two dialogues, *Critias* and *Timaeus*, were regarded as purely legendary, or if highly qualified critics did not consider this matter worth being believed and discussed. Plato was one of our greatest philosophers and a man well known for his love of truth, his balanced judgment and his sincerity. These earned him the name «Divine».

Sources of information about Atlantis are mentioned extensively in *Timeus* and *Critias*. Both dialogues were written in Plato's old age, after his two last stays at Syracuse, when he had already realized the impossibility of fulfilling his political ideal and had devoted his energies to entirely different pursuits. In *Timeus*, one finds his basic mathematical, physical, geological, and physiological theories. Pythagorean doctrines had an enormous influence upon Plato's production. From Pythagoras he took his method of exposition: symbolic, brief, esoteric, sententious, and artificially mysterious. All these we find incorporated in *Timeus*.

Timaeus is Plato's cosmogony. In a production as profound, original and various as Plato's, there had to be a cosmogony and this dialogue has always been considered his masterpiece. It is a veritable encyclopaedia, where all the knowledge of his times is condensed. There he dealt not only with scientific studies, but with all manner of beliefs, even those superstitions which were current in his day.

Four characters have parts of varying importance in *Timaeus:* Socrates, Hermocrates, Critias and Timaeus. The first two only say a few words; the third one offers his already mentioned description of Atlantis, which is pursued at length in *Critias*, a sequel of *Timaeus* which Plato left unfinished. In this last dialogue, he deals again with Atlantis and, in order to compare its organization to that of Athens, the writer offers us a more detailed description of the physical and political characteristics of this country, which ends with a moral justification for its downfall.

(Appendix I in this book is devoted to the history of Atlantis as it appears in *Timaeus* and *Critias*.)

Some of the assertions made by the priest of Sais are worth special attention. What he says supports Hörbiger's theories thus, incidentally, indicating the depth of Egyptian scientific studies.

The priest in *Timaeus* says: «Sometimes, those bodies revolving in space round the Earth, divert from their usual course. Thus, at wide intervals in time, everything upon earth is destroyed by fire... At other times, the gods purify the Earth by means of water, flooding it.»

Hörbiger's central idea is used by the priest to explain the sinking of Atlantis, brought about by the appearance of our present satellite, which was the origin of ceaseless landslides and tremendous volcanic eruptions, together with a rising in the waters of the tropical seas. This ultimately submerged Atlantis. Hörbiger's calculations show that our Moon became attached to the Earth's orbit about 1,000 years ago, and these figures are in agreement with those given by Plato if one adds the 9,600 years which Plato ascribes to the sinking of Atlantis and the 2,500 years that separate us from the Greek philosopher.

In his *A Life History of the Earth*, Bellamy shares Hörbiger's opinion by stating that the sinking of Atlantis may have taken place 12,000 years ago. The Austrian cosmographer, who died in 1931, is also famous for his *Glacialkosmogonie*, a theory about the formation of the solar universe. This theory, however, has not been fully accepted by contemporary scientists such as the French Furon and the English Hoyle. It has, nevertheless, been successfully applied to explain certain scientific enigmas, and it has proved itself specially useful in the analysis and classification of myths, whether having been dated from the dawn of history or still current among the savage tribes nowadays.

Another famous historian, G. Glotz, speaking about the part played by «myths» in historical research, wrote: «It is a universal feature that legend precedes history; but research, when strenuously performed and, above all, when the investigator has recourse to the comparative method, can trace historical elements in the very legends.»

A better understanding of the causes given in the *Glacialkosmogonie* for the sinking of Atlantis will be achieved if one pauses to consider the process by which the moons became attached to the Earth's orbit. This theory demonstrates that the Earth had attracted a whole series of moons and that the main geological periods —Primary, Secondary, and Tertiary— have been brought abruptly to an end by the loss of one of these moons, with a number of catastrophes entailing.

Hörbiger believed that when our present moon entered the Earth's orbit, it attracted the seas and presumably was then closer to our planet than it is now, for an equilibrium in gravitation was only achieved after a series of oscillations. It was then that the waters, which spread towards both poles, were attracted by the moon and flooded Atlantis and other lands in the southern hemisphere.

The theory of how the Moon was attracted to the Earth, maintains that our moon was a small planet which, like all planets, revolved around the sun, following a spiral which grew gradually narrower. Small planets revolve more swiftly than bigger ones round the sun, because their force of inertia is smaller; they carry less power from that original explosion that separated them from the sun. And thus, in their swifter centripetal spiral, the smaller planets overtake the big ones. It becomes inevitable, then, that when a small planet comes too near a big one, the more powerful gravitation of the latter proves stronger than the sun's. The smaller planet starts revolving round the big one and thus becomes its satellite. This is what is believed to have taken place comparatively recently —about 12-13,000 years ago. The Moon is now sixty terrestial radii from the Earth. It will eventually draw nearer, causing a permanent tide under its course's ellipse; it will flood the tropics, save for the highest mountains. All living beings on the Earth will feel their weight less and a new breed of gigantic beasts and men will appear. Novel species of enormous plants will also be born. Drawing nearer still, the Moon will explode and form an immense ring of rocks, ice, water, air, and other gases round the Earth. This ring will tighten its grasp until it finally crashes with the Earth. It could well be the end of mankind, as Hörbiger's calculations indicate that this Moon is clearly bigger than the previous moons, and thus its collapse would be more violent than any of the catastrophes which occurred in the past.

Hörbiger's disciples maintain that there are some fairly precise details of the fall of the Tertiary moon in the *Apocalypse*. H. S. Bellamy, Hörbiger's most brilliant disciple, has now interpreted these passages in the *Apocalypse* in his *The Book of Revelation is History*. Bellamy's central theory asserts that the Apocalypse, in depicting the end of the world, was transposing a medley of vague memories of the disaster that ensued from the fall of the moon during the Tertiary period. As the end of the world will be brought about by the fall of our present Moon, his theory is clearly admissible. Events similar to those that took place at the end of the Tertiary period will happen towards the end of the Quarternary period.

Naturally enough, some of the legends concerned with the destruction of the Atlantis merged with older traditions on the annihilation of the previous world. Men have always tended to moralize on the causes of cosmic affairs and catastrophes. Plato was the first to offer an ethical explanation for the destruction of Atlantis. According to him, men became so wicked that the enraged gods punished them. He tells us

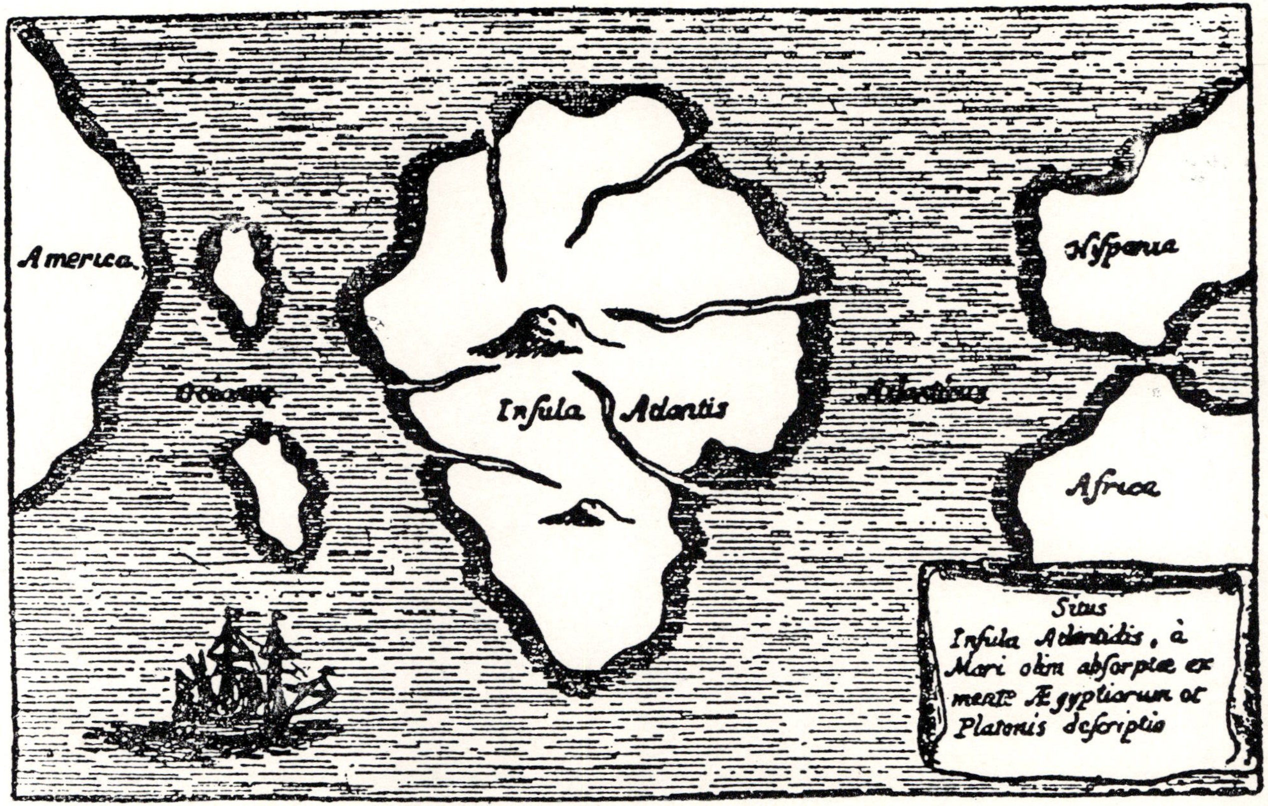

V.—Location of Atlantis, according to Plato's Description.

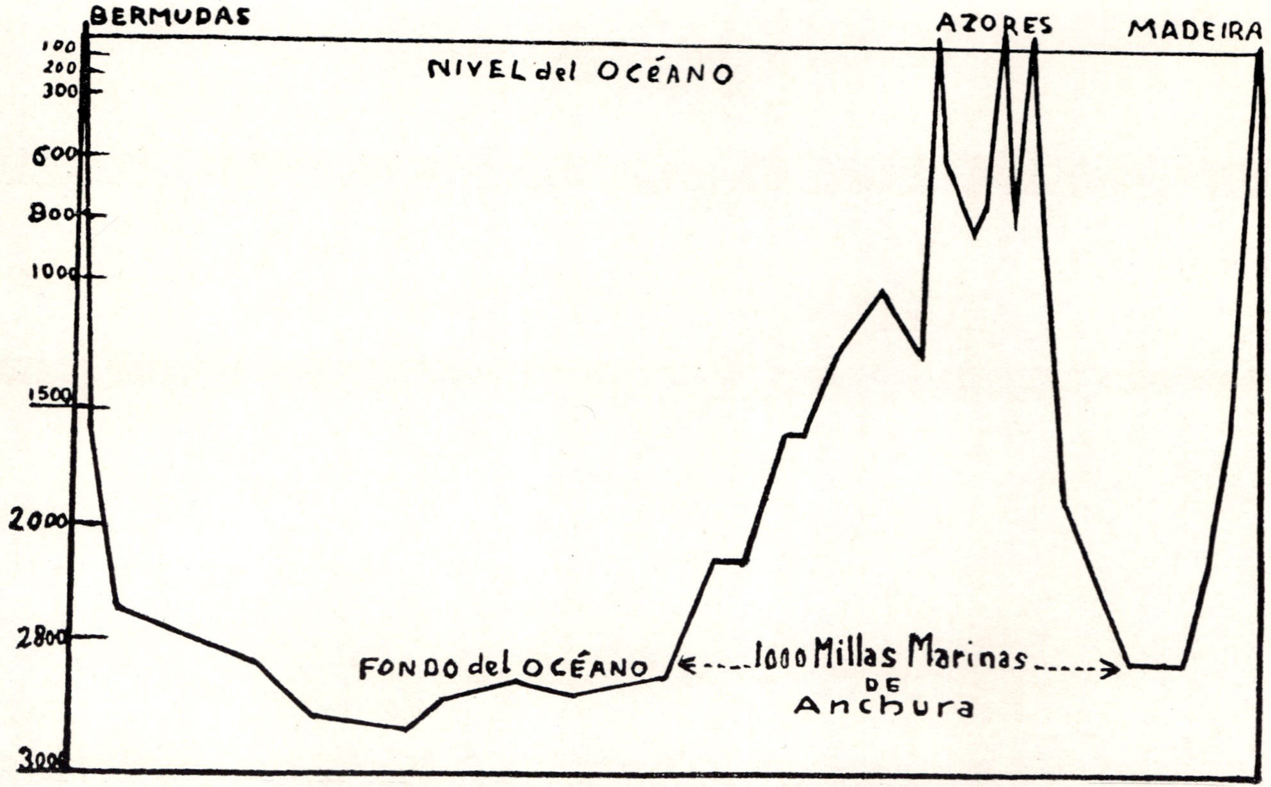

VI.—Contour of the Atlantic Ocean, and of the submerged portion of the ancient island of Atlantis, according to Donnelly.

VII.—Upper section of the huge portico of Tiahuanaco ruins, where the mythical figure and the calendar are carved.

VIII.—Stone heads discovered at the Tiahuanaco ruins.

in *Critias* that: «They practised the grossest indecencies became utterly vile so that Zeus, greatest among the gods, who ruled by the law, realized how evil this breed of men would become, they who had been so excellent at first. So he desired to punish them and thus force them to reflection and induce them to mend their ways.»

Notwithstanding this, Bellamy maintains that corruption followed dissaster, but it did not cause it. Men became evil and cannibalistic because the annihilation of their world ruined and terrified them. Plato himself had said that refinement is destroyed by overwhelming worry over physical needs.

Lastly, it is to be noted that the Egyptians knew about the existence of America; Plato could not have invented it. The priest in *Timaeus* tells us that: «Travellers in those times could cross from one island to all other islands and from them, they could reach the continent which stood on the opposite side of that sea. This kingdom included that island and many other islands and parts of that continent.»

Saurat, in his book *Atlantis*, comments:

«This passage seems to me to prove beyond doubt the superb achievements of Egyptian science —for Plato does not speak again about this continent and he probably does not believe it exists— but it may equally prove the accuracy of the basic points in his narrative: if the Egyptians knew about America and gave its true position in relation to the oceanic islands and Europe-Africa, there is no reason, once Hörbiger's theories are known, to doubt the fundamental truth in the account preserved by Plato.

Who could have invented America? If the Egyptians knew about and were right when speaking of America, what they said concerning Atlantis must have been equally true. These two truths are related. Plato may have made up his description of the old Athenian constitution and that of its islands, but he did not invent America, nor Atlantis. When considering the arguments for and against, Plato's assertions are overriding.

Those in favour of the *Glacialkosmogonie*, among whom we may mention: Georg, Hinzpeter, Fischer, and above all,

Edmund Kiss, are eager to prove that the *Tiahuanaco* structures in the Andes are the remains of one of the colonies of Atlantis. (See Appendix II)

Most of the scholars who have discussed Atlantis agree in accepting Plato's account in its main lines, for it has essentials enough to prove its accuracy. Plato never failed to distinguish the historical and the fictional elements in his work. He insists more than once in *Timaeus* that his narrative is «far from being a literary figment, but a reliable piece of history by all accounts». And when speaking about the heroic prowess of the Athenians in defeating the Atlantes, saving thus their city from the besiegers, Plato pointed out again in *Timeus* that «*This is a feat which, though not very well known, has none the less happened; and there is no doubt whatever about it*».

In his dialogue, Critias calls on the goddess of memory, Mnemosine, and asks her to help him narrate the various events which he wanted to include in his story. And Plato underlined time and again that his account of Atlantis is based on Egyptian inscriptions and papyri which Solon himself saw, so that his narrative is «thoroughly worthy of credit».

But there are other writers who refuse to accept the existence of Plato's Atlantis; so that for them *Timeus* and *Critias* are merely ingenious fables, which Plato invented in order to win the support of tradition for the political system he wanted to establish. Aristotle was the first among these authors to assert that Plato, being unable to put into practice his program for a veritable reorganization of human society, was led to purely poetic imaginings. And thus Aristotle wrote: «Plato alone made Atlantis emerge from the waves, and then he submerged it again».

But Aristotle himself seems to fall into contradictions, according to those who believe Atlantis to be more than a legend, because he wrote in a passage of his *Constitution of the Tegaeians* —preserved by a commentator in Apolonius of Rhodes's *Argonauts*— that the natives of Arcadia in prehelenistic times based their claim to the possession of that land in the fact that they came from Atlantis; and had inhabited their country even before there had been a Moon in the heavens. This last assertion lacked its true sense before Hörbiger's theses.

If we stop to analyse the post-Aristotelian theories about Atlantis, we soon realize that classical authors rarely refer to the Platonic tradition, and when they do it is with the utmost reserve. Roman historians use Greek sources more often than not. The Alexandrian and Roman sources from those times hardly offer any new idea or solution as to the exact position of Atlantis. Notwithstanding this, the Neoplatonist philosopher, Proclus, in his admirable translation with comments of *Timaeus,* tells us that one of Plato's first disciples, Crantor, went to Egypt in order to verify the truth in his master's narrative. And once there, the priests not only proved to him beyond doubt the accuracy of Plato's words, but showed him stele where there were inscriptions describing the history of Atlantis.

Those who dealt with the «question of Atlantis» during the Middle Ages did so but summarily and without granting it any special importance. This was perhaps due not only to Aristotle's influence, who was then the veritable «sun» of philosophy, but also to the fact that the story of Atlantis disagreed with the accounts in the Bible.

In the Modern period, Atlantis was almost completely forgotten. Geopraphers, cartographers, and navigators —that is, all those for whom the subject should have proved attractive— seemed to have never heard about it. Columbus and Toscanelli, for instance, either did not know about it or regarded it as something unworthy of their attention. In the writings of famous navigators, there is not the slightest mention of Plato's island. But this is not surprising when one considers that Columbus probably died without realizing that he had discovered a continent hitherto unknown —at least from an accepted point of view. He always believed that he had arrived at the islands situated in the eastern coast of Asia; hoping to reach Zipangu, Japan, and the mysterious countries described by Marco Polo, by following a shorter route. He never dreamt that between Europe and distant Asia there was a continent, nor the island that Plato had written about. Moreover, it is almost certain that he had never heard about Plato or his «myth», nor about Seneca's prophecy; for otherwise he would have made some mention of it when giving an account of his travels.

It is interesting to remember what a great Latin writer, Seneca, says:

> Venient annis saecula seris
> Quibus Oceanus vincula rerum
> Laxet, et ingens pateat tellus,
> Tethysque novos detegat orbes,
> Nec sit terris ultima Thulé.

> A time will come, after many centuries
> when the oceans, breaking the chains that
> imprison things (which encircle the world)
> will reveal an enormous continent. Then
> Tethys will discover new countries and Thule
> will no longer be the last of the islands
> (the confines of the world)

(SENECA, *Medea*, 376-380)

Seneca, who had a wider knowledge than Columbus and who was, of course, endowed with a finer spirit, could well risk venturing this prophecy in his time. Had he heard about the unknown Marcellus, later quoted by Proclus? And, because of this, did he know of the existence of «those numerous islands, placed beyond the pillars of Hercules», which, if this narrative is true, would be none other than the Azores and the Canaries? In any case, he did know of Ulysses's travels and of his meeting Calypso and dwelling in her cave in the Ogygia island for some time. It is remarkable that in our time, this island has been identified with one of the Canaries because, according to Homer, it had a huge mountain in the midst —this could well be the Teide. Seneca had also read Diodorus of Sicily and thanks to this, he perhaps knew of the fearless Phoenician sailors who had at one time discovered an immense island in the Atlantic Ocean— Cuba or Jamaica, according to some modern authorities. And he perchance learned from Strabo of how many courageous sailors had at that time ventured far towards the West. Be it what it may, he had heard that in that distant, unknown, and mysterious West there were some islands called *Blessed* by the Greeks and *Fortunate* by the Romans. These islands —the Canaries— had already inspired numerous classical poets because of the sweetness of their climate. Among them, Horace delighted in chanting:

> Nos manet Oceanus circum vagus; arva, beata
> Petamus arva, divites et insules,
> Reddit ubi Cererem tellus inarata quitannis.

> The ocean which surrounds the world is
> calling us. Let us sail towards the blessed
> fields of the Fortunate Islands, where every
> year, the soil of Ceres yields its fruits without
> being tilled.

(HORACE, Epod., XVI, 41)

Silence ensued for several centuries, until the question of Atlantis had once again a place in literature, half a century after the discovery of America. With the advent of the Renaissance and the rediscovery of Platonic philosophy, men were once again vitally interested in Atlantis. It was due to this fact that, after such a problematic, uncertain, obscure past, under the ban of Aristotelian philosophy, the «question of Atlantis» regained the place it deserved— managing to imbue a new faith in so many modern authors who nowadays believe in its one-time existence.

After the Renaissance, there was what one could term an impasse in the studies concerning Atlantis until the French astronomer Jean Sylvain Bailly, the author of a *History of Astronomy*, rescued the matter from oblivion, towards the end of the eighteenth century. Bailly was persuaded of the need to allow for the existence of a nation, which had attained its maturity before all the known cultures in History —a nation which had disappeared after having acquired a high degree of civilization, the remains of which, preserved by tradition, were certain astronomical measurements known to several Eastern people, whom he thought incapable of having obtained them by themselves.

Bailly published his famous *Letters on Atlantis* in 1778, three years after his *History of Primitive Astronomy*, and his second book achieved a popularity similar to that of the *Persian Letters*. The French astronomer addressed his famous letters to Voltaire, attempting to prove to his contemporary the existence of a very old civilization beside the Greek, which had and enormous influence upon those cultures which we deem the oldest, such as Brahmanic wisdom, among others. Bailly called Plato as his witness and referred to the history of Atlantis, its kings and its institutions as they appeared in *Timeaus* and *Critias*.

Bailly had addressed his letters on Atlantis to Voltaire wanting, no doubt, to win the approval of a man of unquestioned intellectual reputation. Voltaire said nothing against Baillys theories and from this we may infer that he did agree with them.

Here is a transcription of one of Bailly's letters which, we believe, is particularly interesting.

«Here ends Plato's text; the rest is lacking. But it is clear that the philosopher, in attempting to reap a healthy example for the benefit of men, had prepared to describe the sinking of the island of Atlantis —the annihilation of its inhabitants— as a punishment for their sins. Divine justice destroyed that den from which so many greedy conquerors and depredators had sprung, bringing unhappiness to the world. They became the scourge of the world, and heaven's scourge destroyed the island where they had been born.

No doubt, Plato tried not only to please his readers by his story of the Atlantes, but also to instruct them.

He was more of a moralist than a poet, so he painted with relish their commendable primitive customs, their corruption and their punishment. But it is clear that the moral issue is here no more than accessory. He is a historian, depicting a terrible catastrophe, and reaping from it a moving lesson. He speaks about the virtues of the Atlantes, but he does so in order to emphasize the enormity of their heavenly punishment. If morality had been his basic preoccupation, he would have explained in more detail those healthy customs he hoped to imitate and he would not have given such a great lenght to the minute description of the size and situation of the island, its wealth, and its magnificent palaces and temples.

Everything must bear proportion when inserted in a small picture and thus, these descriptions are long if we take into account the brevity of the narrative. Plato was a master of literary form and knew well how to place his main theme in what we might term a corner of his picture, while dealing at leisure with minor particulars. He invented neither the basic question nor the details and while leaving there the stamp of truth, he would have left his own had he been writing about something fictitious. Plato tells us that the ten chieftains gathered every five or six years at the temple of Neptune, without showing any special preference for odd or even numbers. If Plato had invented these people, or, at least, their beliefs and customs, he —who had built the world according to the five regular geometrical bodies, and based divine perfection and human generation on the number three in his metaphysical cogitations— could not have failed to endow that country he had created with his own ideas. And, moreover, he would not have insulted classical antiquity, sublimely reverent of odd numbers, by attributing to his Atlantes a complete indifference towards those mysterious numbers...

Plato's story... does ring true. It is not a piece of fiction written to amuse or instruct his readers. A further proof of the fact that Plato was only transcribing, not inventing, is that Homer, who lived many years before him and had a wide knowledge of foreign countries and people, mentioned the Atlantes and their island in the *Odyssey*... The name of Atlas and that of the Atlantes is recurrent in all classical writers: Diodorus, Strabo, Pliny, Solon, Euripedes, etc.... Neither the poet nor the philosopher has invented these names; and considering that a thing is named after its existence —this proves the reality of Atlantis. It does not follow that these writers are merely repeating what the philosopher said, for they give many details which are not to be found in Plato's dialogues. So it is plain that there was a historical basis, a tradition remembered; original sources, which were known both to these writers and to Plato. Diodorus of Sicily and Sanchuniathon preserved the genealogies and feats of the heroes of Atlantis; so now I will quote some passages in their narratives for I have to base my assertions on their accounts, and on that offered by Plato. We must remember that we are dealing with an old race, the invasion of the earth, and a great revolution which altered and destroyed everything. I will have to multiply my proofs in order to clarify the events; and I also will have to gather together those details which depict how this momentous event took place. Plato has described Atlantis for us; Diodorus of Sicily will speak about the men who inhabited it. The history of those distant times is not altogether lost; we may find it, though fragmentary and scattered, in the writings of various authors...

(Letter XII to Voltaire
28 February 1778)

In 1882, the American writer and politician, Ignatius Donnelly, published his *The Antediluvian World*, which became quite popular. Here he asserted that the Canary Islands, Madeira, and Azores were the peaks of the mountains of Atlantis. He underlined, above all, the striking similarities found between the ethnography and the earliest civilizations in the old and new worlds. He firmly believed Egypt and Mexico to be colonies established by the old Atlantes, basing this assertion on the resemblance between both cultures.

According to Donnelly, Atlantis had been the point of departure of our present civilization: «To them we owe all that is basic in our ideals about life and the world. They were the first civilizing force, the first sailors, the first tradesmen, the first colonizers and colonists on earth. Their civilization was already old when that of Egypt was young. Their kingdom flourished thousands of years before Babylon, Rome, or London ever existed.»

Donnelly ascribes to the Atlantes a number of discoveries such as the magnetic needle, gunpowder, the manufacturing of silk and paper, the raising of most garden plants, the tillage of fields, and the study of scientific astronomy.

It is interesting to have a look at the synoptic chart which Donnelly included in his book, to understand more clearly why he traced the origins of all these things to the Atlantes.

> 1. Once upon a time, there existed in the midst of the Atlantic Ocean, facing the access to the Mediterranean, a huge island which was what was left of an Atlantic continent. This island was known to the classical world as Atlantis.
>
> 2. The description which Plato gave of this island is not altogether a fabulous legend, as it was believed to be for quite a long time. It is a valuable piece of history concerning the prehistoric period.
>
> 3. Atlantis is the very land where man, for the first time cast off barbarousness and achieved civilization.
>
> 4. The people of Atlantis, in the course of many centuries, became a large and powerful nation, with men enough to spare for colonizing and civilizing the shores off the Gulf of Mexico, those of the Pacific Ocean in South America, the banks of the Mississippi and the Amazon and also, the shores of the Mediterranean, Western Europe, Western Africa, the Baltic, the Black Sea, and the Caspian.
>
> 5. Atlantis was no less than the world itself before the Flood, where the Garden of Hesperides, the Elysium, and Olympos were.
>
> 6. The gods, goddesses, and heroes worshipped by the old Greeks, Phoenicians, Hindus, and Scandinavians were none other than the kings, queens, and heroes of Atlantis; and likewise, the feats and deeds mythology ascribes to them are but vague memories of actual prehistoric events.
>
> 7. Peruvian and Egyptian mythology are an echo of the early religion of Atlantis, where the Sun was adored.

8. The tools and other implements dating from the European Bronze Age came from Atlantis; and the Atlantes were the first to smelt iron.

9. Atlantis was also the earliest place where the Indo-european families settled.

10. Atlantis was destroyed by a terrible catastrophe which made it sink into the sea, leaving above the water only the highest peaks —which are now the archipelagos of the Canaries, the Azores, Cape Verde, etc.— and annihilating almost all its inhabitants.

11. Only a few men could save themselves in boats or rafts. They carried the news of the appalling disaster to the people settled along the Eastern and Western shores of the ocean. The memory of this event has been preserved until our own times in many of the countries in both continents where it is referred to as: the FLOOD.

In 1888, the Russian writer, H. P. Blavatsky, in her *The Secret Doctrine*, asserted that Atlantis would be considered the first historical continent if more attention were given to the old traditions. The famous island, to which Plato gave its name, would be but part of that original continent. Saurat points out that one cannot disregard what Mrs. Blavatsky had to tell about her Tibetan and Hindu sources —sources of an immense antiquity and through which she attempted to give the most important dates in the history of mankind, the influence exerted by the moon, abnormal growth and its degenerations, etc. Her writings become greatly valuable considering that in them we find the ideas and beliefs of the Tibetans which are clearly connected with the hypotheses of the Viennese scholar, Hörbiger.

The authenticity of Plato's narrative had been heatedly championed until the middle years of our century. Many researchers have tried to solve the enigma of Atlantis. According to Ceram, more than 20,000 volumes have been written about Atlantis. Braghine estimates the number to be closer to 25,000. Bessmertny asserts, and not without reason, that: «Plato, with his narrative about Atlantis, flung a pebble into a vacuum, which has caused a veritable avalanche of theories». No means have been spared in the attempt to unveil, even if only partially, this mystery. Societies have been founded, expeditions organized, and conferences held with only this subject for discussion.

The paramountcy of this matter is such that a magazine, *Atlantis*, appeared in 1926. It is still being published and not only does it collect whatever deals with the «lost continent» but also investigates all that concerns that primitive civilization.

The beautiful legend of Atlantis which the famous disciple of Socrates unfolded, and which has inspired so many poets, among them the Spanish Verdaguer, seems to have acquired nowadays an increased attraction, not only for men of letters, but for scientists as well.

CHAPTER III

Prehistoric Times

1.—Legendary Times

2.—Origin of the Name of the Canary Islands

3.—Phoenician, Carthaginian, and Roman Expeditions

4.—Origin of the Guanches, their Physical Characteristics and their Mingling with the other Races

5.—Analogies Between the Guanches and the Cro-Magnon Race

6.—Spreading of the Cro-Magnon Race over Europe and its Settlement in the Canary Islands

7.—Persistence of the Guanche Type in the Present Population of the Canary Islands

1.—LEGENDARY TIMES

Classical antiquity did remember the archipelago of the Canaries, and though in these remote times the history of the island proper was not known, the Greeks had already traced the legendary history of this unique land in their allegories and myths. We have, for instance, the legend of Atlas, the king of Mauritania, who gave his name to the Western seas and the great mountain range of the African continent. He married Hesperis and had seven daughters —the Hesperides or the Atlantes who suffered grievous captivity in the oceanic islands.

One of the famous labours of Hercules, so often sung by the poets, was precisely the release of the daughters of Atlas. And the spoils of this victory were the golden apples taken from the garden of Hesperides. This explains why the Canary Islands, because of their part in this memorable feat, were given the classical names of Hesperides or Atlantes.

The Fortunate Islands have had the privilege of being regarded as the Garden of Eden and the oceanic palace ever since the earliest times —their beauties described by Homer, Horace, Silius, Italicus, Diodorous of Sicily, Florus, Tibullus, Pliny, and many other classical writers.

Proteus depicts to Menelaus this peerless land as the most peaceful place on earth where men may chose to end their days. Virgil takes Aeneas and the Sibyl to these merry *places* and *quiet gardens* in the fortunate woods, where they meet *the glorious souls of those who suffered terrible wounds in fighting for their country, those of priests who led chaste lives, and those of the prophets who predicted things worth of Phoebus.*

In his lovely stories, Diodorus of Sicily, gave these islands the name of Hesperides, where plenty of cattle and delicious

55

fruits were found. Pindar also sang their splendour. The great Canarian poet, Cairasco, harmoniously merged all the legends about the Canary Islands with true historical facts in his poem *El Arco de la Fama:*

> Otras islas se ven que el blanco velo
> Las ciñe en torno, menos elevadas,
> Llamólas por su fértil cielo y suelo
> La antigua edad las islas Fortunadas;
> Y tan amigo suyo estimo el cielo
> Que de su voluntad no cultivadas,
> Las tierras entendió dar nobles frutos,
> Y las incultas vides sus tributos.
> Siempre decía florecer la oliva,
> Destilar de las piedras miel sabrosa,
> Y con murmullo blando el agua viva
> Bajar del alto monte presurosa;
> Templar el aire la calor estiva,
> De suerte que a ninguna es enojosa,
> Y en fin por su templanza, lauros, palmas,
> Ser los Campos Elísees de las almas.

In traslation it is read as:

> Other smaller islands are seen, surrounded
>   by this white veil,
> Antiquity called them, because of the fertility
>   of their soil and sky, Fortunate Islands;
> And so friendly towards them was heaven
> That without any labouring, the earth yielded
>   wonderful fruits
> An the uncultivated vines offered their tribute.
> It was said that olive trees always flowered,
> And sweet honey dripped from the stones,
> And with a soft rumour lively waters hurried
>   down the steep mountainside;
> A summery warmth mellowed the air, so that
>   pleasure reigned,
> And lastly, because of their temperateness,
>   laurels and palms, they were the Elysium
>   of the souls.

2.—The Origin of the Name of the Canary Islands

In Genesis and in the Book of Ezekiel, the Canary Islands are called the islands of Elysa or Elysia, from where hyacinth and purple came —a fact which also afforded them the name of Purpurarias (Purple Islands).

The name of Hesperides, which was also given to these islands, is interesting too. But one has to take into account that Hesperia was the name given to all the western countries.

The Canaries could also have been the Garden of Hesperides, where wild orange trees grew all the year round. This theory was considered inaccurate, on thinking that such trees had not reached the Canaries until after the conquest, but it regained credence when Viera y Clavijo discovered that among the fossilized leaves found, there were many belonging to orange trees.

Canary Islands has been the name which has prevailed, and there are various theories about its origin.

Viera y Clavijo tells us that the vassals of the Italian kings, Cranus and Crana, set to sea in search of adventure and arrived in these islands. They settled in one of them and named it *Cranaria*, in memory of their princes. When the Spaniards arrived, they preserved that name but adapted it to their own language, modifying it to *Canary*.

A hypothesis more in accordance with the poet's temperament was ventured, to be forgotten afterwards, by Viera y Clavijo himself who says that *Canarias* derived its name from the Latin verb *Cano* which means «to sing», and *canorous*, as it is generally believed that canary birds, known for the beauty of their song, are native to the Canary Islands. Jacob Savary, on the other hand, states that the birds took their name from the islands and not vice versa.

The theory more widely accepted now is that the name *Canary* was derived from the huge dogs that the explorers sent by King Juba found in the islands of Gran Canaria.

But perhaps the most logical and simple theory is the one accepted by Viera, who attributed this name to the enormous stir caused by the conquest of Gran Canaria —the name of which absorbed those of the other islands and became so widespread that it was generally given to all those islands, which had been known as Fortunate until the fifteenth century.

Roman historians gave these islands Latin names: Canaria to Gran Canaria, Nivaria to Tenerife, Capraria to Lanzarote, Pluvialia or Ombrion to El Hierro, Planaria to Fuerteventura, Junonia Mayor to La Palma, and Junonia Menor to La Gomera.

King Juba and Pliny, the naturalist, spoke only of six islands. The Canarian scholar and philologist, Alvarez Delgado, identifies them as follows: Ombrion would be the Gran Salvaje, Junonia - La Palma, Junonia Menor - La Gomera, Caprania - El Hierro, Nivaria - Tenerife, and Canaria - Gran Canaria. According to the aformentioned scholar, Lanzarote and Fuerteventura did not appear on the list because Juba and Pliny called them the Purpurarias or Purple Islands.

3.—Phoenician, Carthaginian, and Roman Expeditions

In all countries, history is preced by legend. The Canary Islands, the supposed remains of the immense continent sunk at the dawn of the world, also have their mythical age, preceding the expeditions which claim to have visited the islands in classical antiquity.

Hesperus peopled the Fortunate Islands and Hercules helped him support the celestial sphere. This fate was given Hercules for having stolen the golden apples from the islands of Hesperides, killing the dragon which guarded them. Some people believe that this dragon, as Viera y Clavijo asserts, was inspired by the dragon-tree —a tree native to these islands whose trunks resembles a serpent and whose sap looks like blood, two characteristics apt to transform it into a fabulous monster.

The Asiatic civilizations and traditions dating from the most distant ages had already known of the existence of a continent called Atlantis. Plato mentioned it in his writings, and it is now presumed that the Canary Islands, Madeira, and the archipelagos of Azores and Cape Verde were once part of this continent.

In these early times, the Greeks gathered their exact knowledge of the Canaries from the Phoenicians and, as both of them were venturesome people, it is not hard to believe that they sailed past the Pillars of Hercules and visited the Canary Islands. But these are mere suppositions, without corroborative evidence, and only serve to show the poetic imagination of the Greeks, who probably were most inspired by the spirit of these Proenicians. It has also been surmised that the Greeks, inspired by the Phoenicians, placed the eternal dwelling of their heroes in the Elysium.

Diodorus of Sicily spoke of an island standing to the West and situated far from the Libyan shores. The seafaring and industrious Phoenicians had wanted to settle in them also, but they were prevented from doing so by the Carthaginians who wanted the islands for themselves. Hesiodus called these islands Fortunate Islands; Strabo gave them the name of Blessed (Bienaventuradas) Islands and the Esenians, an austere Hebrew sect devoted to contemplation, placed Paradise in some islands which were believed to be the Canaries. In classical antiquity they were called Elysian and Hesperides. The Romans called them Fortunate because of their mild climate and rich vegetation.

It has not been wholly proved which expedition was the first to arrive in the islands. There are details, however, in the famous voyage undertaken by the Phoenicians under the orders of Nekao, a king who had his court at Sais, leading us to believe that these sailors were the first visitors of the Canary Islands.

Nekao's curiosity to know whether Libya was surrounded by the sea except where an isthmus joins it to Asia, sent' these courageous seamen in such an interesting voyage. It is well known that in old times the sailing course was marked by the proximity of the coastline and, hence, once they sailed past Cape Juby, they entered the channel that divided the African coast from the western group of the Canaries. It seems natural that, being so near those islands, they would draw away from the dry African beaches and seek a much needed rest in the pleasant Canaries.

It is now beyond doubt that the Phoenicians did not restrict their sailing and enterprising genius to becoming the kings of the Mediterranean. They travelled past the famous Pillars of Hercules, discovering new countries and trading with them, which was the end they pursued. It was highly convenient for them to keep quiet about those feats, but their renowned courage in those affairs, the geographical position of the archipelago, and the purple, which is not only obtained from sea shells but also from the orchilla, a wild plant of the Canaries, all these facts make their visit to our islands highly probable.

After defeating Carthage, her rival, Rome kept the maritime power of the vanquished republic. The Romans, however, were not spurred by the spirit of adventure which had characterized the Phoenicians. Sertorius heard about those happy islands from some sailors who had just been there. Charmed by the description and also considering their remoteness an advantage to escape his enemies, he probably came to these islands. Lucius Flaccus stated that he landed in the Canaries when his fleet was scattered by a storm off the Lusitanian coast.

4.—ORIGINS OF THE GUANCHES, THEIR PHYSICAL CHARACTERISTICS AND THEIR MINGLING WITH OTHER RACES

The Guanche race, which had a marked predominance in Tenerife, was to be found in all the islands and must be regarded as that of the primitive inhabitants of the archipelago. Some historians believe them to be of Egyptian origin because of the similarity in the methods of mummifying corpses. Others are more in favour of a Scandinavian or Carthaginian origin, in view of the frequent sea voyages undertaken by these people.

Finally, some authors regard the Guanches as indegenous, that is, as part of the original inhabitants of the lost Atlantis. This last theory has won many supporters of late, as it is now believed that this controversial continent could have actually existed.

According to the most widely accepted theory, we may assert that the race to which these primitive people belonged to was that of Cro-Magnon, for the predominant type among them was of that race.

The Guanches were very tall, the men measuring between five feet nine and six feet two inches. The men of Fuerteventura, with an average height of six feet, are the tallest we know about. The chaplains of Bethencourt recorded how a veritable giant was killed in an attack on a village, where the islanders suffered greatly at the hands of the invaders:

«In it (the attack), ten died. Among them there was a giant nine feet tall. The Sire of Bethencourt had expressly forbidden his men to kill him, and had wanted to capture him alive, if possible; but they said they could not avoid killing him, for he was so strong and fought so well that if they had spared him, they would have risked being taken prisoners and killed.»

According to early authors, the aborigines had clear, rosy skins; fair hair, like that of the mummys, and blue eyes. The skull was elongated, clearly dolichocephalic, showing a marked frontal development, a noble forehead. The face was short, very wide in the upper half and growing narrower in the lower half. The nose was medium-sized, straight, short, and wide, but not flattened. Some of the bones, too, offered special characteristics. The femur, for instance, was the thickest Broca had measured.

The extraordinary strength of this race and the vigour of their organisms was seen in the skeletons found, in the thickness of the bones, and in the deep marks left by the muscles. The Guanches were proportioned, sturdy, and harmoniously featured. The numerous skeletons preserved in several museums in the Canary Islands, above all in the Museo Municipal in Santa Cruz de Tenerife, show that they were exceedingly tall and powerfully built. Likewise, the chroniclers who went with Bethencourt's expedition said that nowhere in the world could there have been found a more beautiful race.

Fathers Bontier and Le Verrier, the historians who recounted Bethencourt's expedition, wrote: «You may travel all over the world and you will not find anywhere people more handsome or graceful than these islanders, both men and women, who would have rather fine minds too, if anyone took the trouble of educating them.»

The early inhabitants mixed with another Semitic race mainly in Gran Canaria, Palma, and Hierro. In all the other islands, this new race constituted a minority, and in Gomera no trace of it has been found. In height, these people were between five foot five and five foot seven inches tall. If sturdiness was the principal feature of the Guanches, a slender frame and head were the main characteristics of these other people.

Another racial type, which has awakened little attention yet, presented a short skull and a wide nose. It mixed with the two described above, and constituted a small minority of the indegenous population in Gran Canaria and Hierro, though in Gomera, where no Semitic element was found, this type was rather widespread.

The third ethnical element in the Canaries cannot be referred to any known people. It is perhaps to this unidentified race that a peculiar type of burial is to be ascribed, namely the placing of corpses in graves without mummifying them, instead of using natural or artificial caves for this purpose, as was the general procedure.

All in all, it may be said that the Guanches and their descendants were endowed with extraordinary strength and nimbleness, which they exercised in a great number of sports; and their outdoor life —their dwellings consisted of open caves more often than not— helped them to enjoy an enviable good health.

5.—ANALOGIES BETWEEN THE GUANCHES AND THE CRO-MAGNON RACE

Once the characteristics of the quaternary race of Cro-Magnon were fixed, after the discoveries made in 1868 in the Vézére river (Dordogne) and the finding of five skeletons by Messrs. Berton-Meyron and Delmarés in the cave or shelter which gave its name to this race, it became clear that the Guanches belonged to this type. According to Doctor R. Verneau, all the characteristics presented by the Guanches are precisely those of the Cro-Magnon.

The cavemen of Vézére belonged to the same race that populated the Canary Islands: strong, endowed with the features that denoted an intellectual superiority, nomadic —they hunted great mammals with weapons made of stone, industrious—they manufactured objects made of bone and horn, tanned hides, and adorned themselves with necklaces and bracelets made of fossils, shells, teeth of wild animals, pebbles, and grains of clay; they also made rudimentary earthen vessels and carved with flint tools, showing their powerful artistic instinct in their carved silhouettes of men and beasts.

6.—THE SPREADING OF THE CRO-MAGNON RACE OVER EUROPE AND ITS SETTLEMENT IN THE CANARY ISLANDS

The Cro-Magnon race which lived in the southwest of France from the beginnings of the Quaternary Age, in the second half of the reindeer age, suffered profound changes due to contacts with new people who polished stones, built dolmens, and tamed beasts. Aside from this modification in their lifestyle, the changes in the European climate deprived them of some fundamental resources: with the disappearance of the glaciers, a number of animals which needed cold temperatures migrated. Such was the case with the chamois, which settled in the mountains, and the reindeer which, not being a mountain beast, moved towards the north.

There were plenty of migrations during this period. A number of tribes of the Cro-Magnon race travelled in different directions from the aforesaid center. Those who went towards the southwest and the southeast left their imprint in the Pyrenees and near Marseilles. Their craniological characteristics may be seen in the Basques. They arrived in Italy, crossing the Maritime Alps, and in the north of Africa before the Roman period. Megalithic burials in Tunis, Algeria, and Morocco prove this.

7.—Persistence of the Guanche Type in the Present Population of the Canary Islands

A comparison between the characteristics of the primitive race, based on the remains hitherto analyzed and those of the present population, shows the persistence of the original characteristics and ascertains the preservation of the old racial type. This had been proved by Sabín Berthelot, who took as specimens for comparison some islanders of undoubted Guanche origin. These islanders exceptionally preserved their early names: Bencomo, Pelinor, Doramas, etc. Berthelot thus wrote:

«We had the opportunity more than once to study the Guanche type in people whose origin offered no doubt to us, for they were descendants of the indigenous princes. They came from the *Bencomo*, the *Pelinor*, and the *Doramas*, and they had preserved the name of their ancestors and the pride of that old race. Our minute research showed us a very definite type that presented itself whenever we found new specimens for comparison.

These racial characteristics which have been kept for centuries, from generation to generation, leaving a permanent imprint, appear both in these islands and in those countries where the people of the Canaries migrated to. Thus, not very long ago, we have observed these very features in a South American who closely resembled one of the men we had met in Tenerife and who happened to be a descendant of the old Guanches.»

The purest Guanche type was to be found in Tenerife, and even now it is preserved in many families. Doctor Verneau discovered both the height and all the other physical characteristics in quite a number of individuals. The vast majority of the inhabitants of the other islands are also tall, strong, sturdy, fair-haired, thus preserving the same racial features.

The forceful character of these people has been underlined by all those authors who have written about them. Their natural strength of body and soul —these two combined energies which doubled their physical and spiritual prowess— enabled the Guanches to face any danger, to withstand the worst calamities, to spurn pain in the midst of the most grievous sufferings, and even to survive the very disaster that spelled inevitable death. Viana said that the Guanches:

> Tenían todos por la mayor parte
> Magnánimo valor, altivo espíritu,
> Valientes fuerzas, ligereza y brío;
> Dispuesto talle, cuerpo giganteo:
> Rostros alegres, graves y apacibles,
> Agudo entendimiento, gran memoria,
> Trato muy noble, honesto, y agradable,
> Y fueron con exceso apasionados
> Del amor y provecho de su patria.

Most of them were / Boldly courageous, had noble souls, / Great strength, nimbleness, and spirit; / A handsome gait, gigantic body: / Their faces merry, grave, and serene / Deep intelligence and great memory, / Their manners dignified, decorous, and pleasant, / And they were exceedingly passionate / In their love towards their country.

(VIANA, *Song I*)

Very definite anthropological and ethnographic traces of this primitive people and their culture may be found in the present population, in spite of climatic influences and the fusion of races due to foreign invasions and the general advances of civilization. One must be alert to find in modern nations those characteristics which distinguished them in the earliest historical times, albeit some minor changes which appear in varying proportions:

«Thus we see, even now, the physiognomy uses and habits of the Guanches among the islanders. They have lost their language, of which they have only kept some words; but they still imitate the Guanches in their customs and have preserved their habits and their manners. They are as friendly and as generous, and also know when to be humble and wily. They pass from extreme joy to utter sadness; bold to the point of temerity in the worst perils; they may be shy in the face of some trifling event. They love to gamble, sing, and dance; and are passionately fond of all sorts of gymnastic contests. Grave in their demeanour, simple in their tastes, quiet in their words, cautious, such are the peasants of the Canary Islands, whether they live in a village or in the isolation of a cave or in the mountains. Sincere hospitality, deep respect for their elders, a profound love for their family and mankind in general —those are the virtues the Guanches handed down to their descendants. We, ourselves, have seen how poor goatherds have, in their squalid huts, partaken of their «gofio» and their milk with a stranger asking in return nothing but a blessing for their children. No sooner does the islander see his aged father that he reins his mule, dismounts, and kneels to kiss his hands. Here we have those *barbarians who were endowed with so many natural virtues and simplicity,* as one of our old chroniclers writes with such touching candour. When viewing the history of humanity, the fact that this ancestral goodness still subsists in our modern society is no small consolation. Such appealing qualities have spread, together with the blood of a pure race.

The most moving vignette of this traditional hospitality among the islanders is perhaps to be found in the pages of Eduardo Zamacois, who wrote:

«One evening, towards the all-enveloping hour of sunset, idleness and the exquisite pleasure of walking alone had led me to the road that goes to Taganana. The dying sun melted in gory splendour; a number of anchored vessels rolled on the violet surface of the sea: warships, merchantmen, sailing ships, displayed their magnificent rigging; pleasure and racing yachts, colliers... sitting on the rocks, not far from where I stood, a beggar was eating. He was an old man and his meal, which ho had perhaps obtained at the nearby Engineer Barracks, was probably cold.

I was admiring the view; and no doubt moved by the beauty of that fading evening, I said something aloud... The beggar

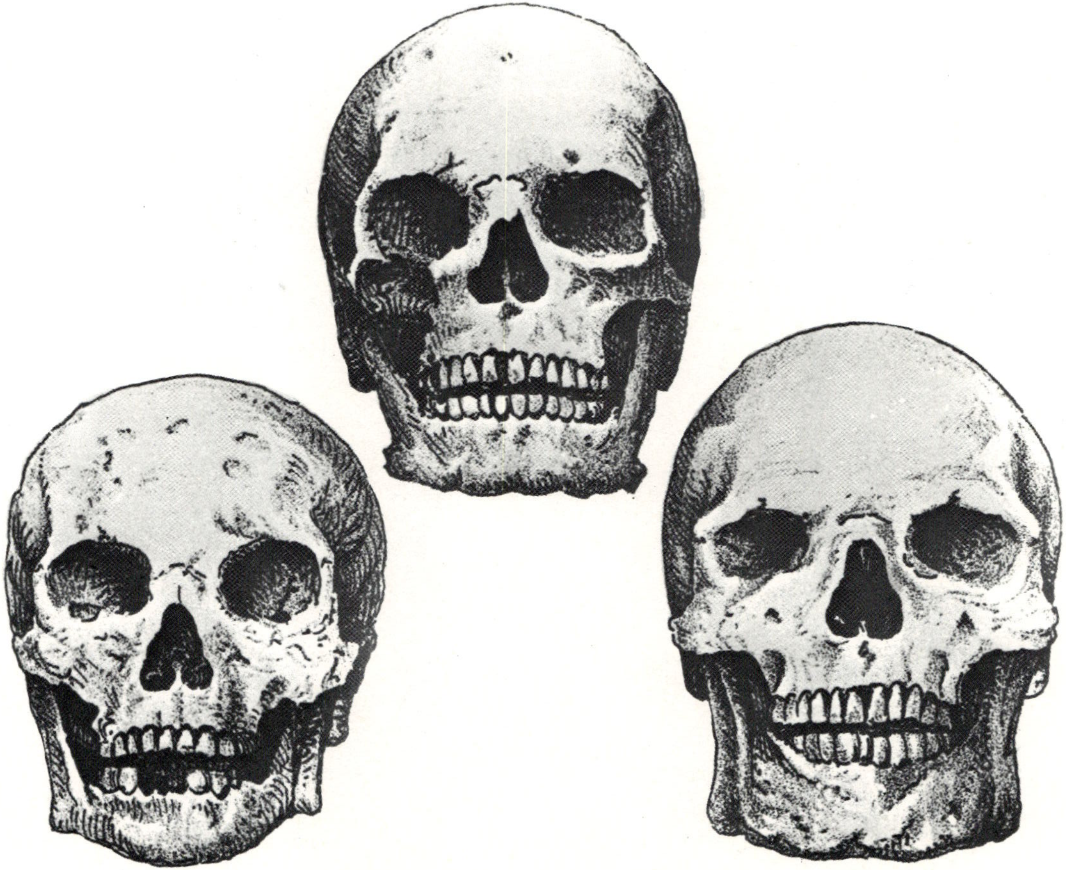

IX.—Mummified Guanche heads, taken from various burial caves.

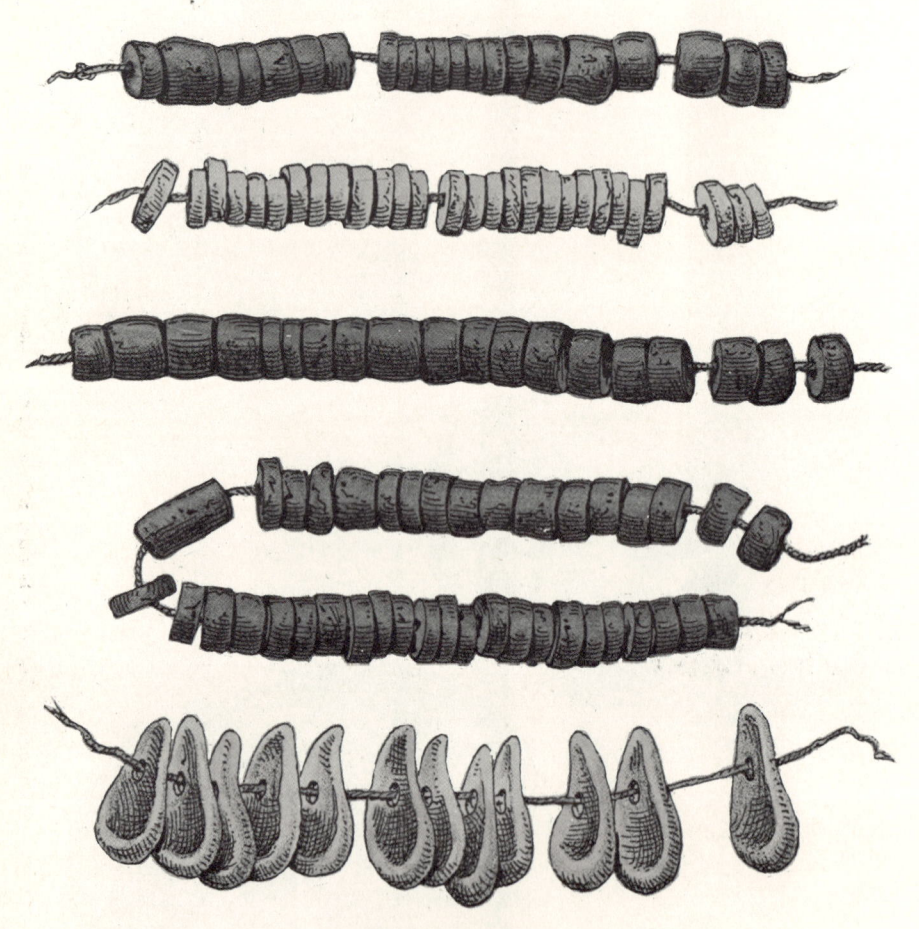

X.—Necklaces worn by the Guanches. They were made from terra-cotta beads and sea-shells.

could not take his eyes off me. We were alone, completely alone. The only audience for the vast theatre of Nature; the sun, like a sublime actor at the end of his daily drama, seemed to be setting only for us, the beauty of his death a peerless offering...

Suddenly, the beggar, forgetting about his destitution, said:
— «It's beautiful, the evening, don't you think?»
— «Very beautiful», I answered.
We remained silent for a short while; the waves broke on the shore, as if rocking the earth.
— «Are you a foreigner?» he asked.
— «I am, indeed.» I replied, «and I come from many and very distant lands...
And on hearing these words, to which I had perhaps given a note of sadness, of disillusionment, he offered me his poor meal and asked me compassionately:
— «Would you like to share this with me?»

I felt deeply touched by his words; pity and gratitude brought tears to my eyes. That man who was offering me what charity had given him, was the symbol, the spokesman for the land I was visiting; and his offer, prompted by twenty centuries permeated by the Gospels, had the majesty, the peacefulness of the evening.

Santa Cruz de Tenerife! You always leave in the wandering souls the soft melancholy that compels one to look back and return to you...

CHAPTER IV

Canarian Civilization in Pre - Conquest Days

1.—Language

2.—Food

3.—Dress

4.—Social Hierarchy

5.—Industry

6.—Marriage

7.—Religion

8.—Public Holidays and Festivals

9.—Weapons

10.—The Mencey's Coronation

11.—Housing

12.—Mummification

13.—Law

14.—A Whistled Language

1.—LANGUAGE

One of the most valuable facts that demonstrates the common origin of all the inhabitants of the islands is the similarity of the languages they spoke. Their vocabulary stemmed from the same source, as word-structure shows in those terms that have been preserved. *Guan* or *Guanche,* for instance, meant «man» in Tenerife. In Gran Canaria, *guanarteme* was used for «king», *arteme* or *artemi* was the name of one of the islands' old sovereigns. «God» received the name *Aborá* in La Palma, *Achaman* in Tenerife, and *Alcorac* in Gran Canaria. *Tamarco,* used to refer to a certain fur garment, was a word common to all the islands. This is the case with a fair amount of terminology. The inflections *ta, gua,* and others, were also found to be of general use as prefixes in a good number of words. Another characteristic shared by all the islanders was their good physical form, together with their deep natural intelligence.

2.—FOOD

Frugality was one of the virtues these primitive people possessed. Only on special occasions, such as their banquets or *guatativoas,* did they equitably share and voraciously consume vast amounts of roasted meat. They did not eat bread but «gofio» or barley flour instead. To obtain this kind of flour, they built hand-worked grinders, of such a rare perfection and delicate design that it seems almost impossible to believe that they were made without recourse to chisels, or other similar iron implements.

The only fruits they knew were the wild ones, and their favourites were the *yoyas* or *mocanes,* from which they extracted the juice they used in kneading the *gofio.* They also ate fish and seafood; their fishing consisted of diving into the water carrying lighted torches. This frightened away their prey and drove them instead into reed nets. It is remarkable that, at that time, the art of swimming was unknown in Tenerife, so the fishes had to be captured by means of goat-horn hooks.

Hierro was the only island to possess the secret of the distillation an alcoholic liquour made from wild fruits. Water and, sometimes, palm-juice, were the only drinks in all the other islands.

3.—Dress

Their garments were made of chamois leather, for cotton and flax were unknown to them; nor did they know the art of spinning the wool from the sheep they reared. This dress was called *tamarco,* which both men and women wore alike —the only difference being that the women wore under it a kind of skirt that reached to their feet, which they took great care to cover for showing them, or their breasts, was considered immodest. The *tamarco* was a robe fastened in front or down one of the sides. The skins, once cut, were held together by very thin strips of goat guts in dainty seams. The artistry of these garments was surprising, considering that they had no needles and had to use awls made of fish bone or palm thorns. They wore leather sandals fastened to the leg by thin straps. Necklaces were made of earthenware beads of different shapes, sea shells, and carved bones.

Their industry was as scarce as their physical needs. Metals were totally unknown to them and thus, in this respect, their civilization was a primitive as that of the people who had lived during the Stone Age. Because of their isolation, and the characteristics of the land they inhabited, they were unable to outgrow this stage.

4.—Social Hierarchy

The main symbol of wealth was the possession of a greater or smaller number of cattle. This ownership, which was thought to be of divine origin, was almost exclusively in the hands of the nobility, who had slaves or commoners as servants.

XI.—Typical Garafía costumes, Island of La Palma.

XII.—Banana trees and girls dressed in the typical Tazacorte costume, Island of La Palma.

XIII.—The National Park at the Caldera de Taburiente, Island of La Palma.

XIV.—The snow-covered peak of the Teide.

Núñez de la Peña gives us a threefold division of these social classes: the nobility, whom he calls *achimenceyes;* the squires or *cinchiciquizes*, and the villains or *archicaxnas*. The king was the owner by right of all agricultural land, but it was his duty to distribute it annually among his vassals, according to their rank and the services they had rendered. The *faican* or high priest was second in authority and it was he who created the new nobility and conferred the dignity of knighthood. The distinctive signs of knighthood were a thick beard and hair worn down to the ears. When a candidate was to be thus honoured, he had first to prove the nobility of his origins and also his expert handling of arms. The *faican* then publicly asked the assembly, who had previously gathered, whether someone had seen the candidate entering the pen to milk or slaughter goats, or cooking his meals with his own hands, stealing in times of peace, or being rude and foul-mouthed, especially to a woman. More often than not, the answer was in the affirmative; then the unlucky and unhappy candidate was declared a villain forever; his hair shorn and then nicknamed *trasquilado*. But if he successfully passed the test, his hair was cut just to his ears and he was made a member of this very noble order.

5.—INDUSTRY

Cloth, though manufactured with rare ingenuity, offered nothing remarkable. Most of it was made from reeds and vegetable fibres or palms, and it seemed to have been used only to make mats, baskets, or fishing tackles.

Pottery was a more progressive industry. Even nowadays, this primitive industry, using the same Guanche techniques, still flourishes in some parts of the islands. Almost always, the objects manufactured by these modern potters are given their old Guanche names. The primitive potters did not have access to the wheel or any other similar device. They worked and shaped the clay manually. Then, the piece of pottery was left to dry for a day, before it was finished. When almost dry, it was carefully polished by means of very smooth stones, which were easily found in all the beaches in the islands. Sometimes they also used bones for polishing. As a rule, all these objects had no decorations, and only rarely do we find some kind of ornament in them. When decorated, the design was done manually and with a linear pattern.

Not only did they make utensils for domestic use, but beads of various shapes and sizes for necklaces. They must have been very fond of this type of ornaments, for a good number of them have been found in their caves.

6.—MARRIAGE

In Gran Canaria, as in Sparta, it was thought of primary importance for women to be strong enough to bear sturdy sons who could be of service to their nation.

Thus, those maidens who were about to marry retired to their chamber for thirty days before the wedding. There they ate rich food, which prevented them from being repudiated, or so they thought. But in all the other islands, not even this requisite was needed; it was enough that both spouses agreed to have the marriage celebrated. Likewise, it was only necessary for both of them to be of one accord in order to have it dissolved, after which, the two of them were free again to marry whomever they pleased. These divorces and remarriages never gave rise to quarrels or rancour. The only evil they entailed was the fact that the sons born from annulled marriages were considered illegitimate. It is remarkable that, as a result of this general free will among the islanders, the women of Gran Canaria and Lanzarote were generally married to three husbands, who enjoyed their married bliss on alternate months.

7.—RELIGION

The islanders obscurely believed in an Almighty and Eternal Being. This divine spirit was the object of all their worship, and was given a physical representation in some islands. The stone idol, discovered during the reign of Alfonso IV of Portugal by some seamen from that country who came to these islands, is an example. Religious rituals varied from island to island. In Gran Canaria, this god was worshipped at the summits of the mountains or in small chapels, which were tended by the *Magnadas* —vestal virgins dressed in white skins and famous for their modesty and piety. In La Palma, they built high stone pyramids in honour of Aborá (God) and danced round them. In Lanzarote, they offered him milk jugs which they poured on the mountain peaks. A similar offering was made in the temples of Fuerteventura. Tradition says that in this last island there lived two women called *Tamonante* and *Tibabrin,* who could forsee future events, and uttered their vaticinations in prophetic tones accompanied by convulsive gestures. This won them the utmost prestige and veneration throughout the country. The people from Hierro were no less superstitious, for they believed that this god descended from heaven to hear their prayers, and that he stood on two high rocks which were then called *Eraorahan* and *Mereiba*. They are presently called *Santillos de los Antiguos*.

The people from Tenerife believed in an evil being whom they called *Guayota*. They thought hell was located at the Teide Volcano, whose eruptions filled them with religious terror. But they also believed in a benign being who dwelt in the heavens and whose help they asked with ardent entreaties in times of need. Even beasts took part in their religious cults, for they took lambs and kids away from their mothers in the belief that the bleatings of these were supplications most welcome to the divinity.

8.—Public Holidays and Festivals

Nothing is more telling of a people than the manner in which they choose to amuse themselves. The merry inhabitants of Gran Canaria were known for their magnificent dancing and the sweetness of their music. The robust Tenerife Guanches, on the other hand, being more warlike and rough, preferred to show off their enormous strenght in wrestling and by jumping over deep ravines and terrifying precipices.

Harvest time or *Beñasmen* constituted the most important annual festivity. Public banquets were held. Then, together with wrestling and other amusements, they celebrated lavishly. If the tribes were at war, hostilities ceased for the time being. This truce was so faithfully respected that even those belonging to a state at war could visit other territories, in the certainty of suffering no danger.

9.—WEAPONS

War weapons were made of wood or stone. They were used as missiles and the natives expertly threw and dodged them. Their emblems of command were also simple wooden staffs. They also had very sharp stones called *tabonas*, which they employed as cutting instruments and with which they could perform such delicate incisions that they had recourse to them for bleeding people.

Axes had edges made of a piece of obsidian. Spears were of wood hardened by fire. They also had mastered the art of throwing the javelin and used the *banot*, a kind of deadly dart, which was carved in such a way that one of its notches held onto the wound as the handle sank into the flesh. They had shields made from the bark of the dragon-tree.

But when the fight started and before engaing in a hand-to-hand combat with their foes, stones were their principal weapons and their main missiles, whether they threw them by means of a sling, as Viana tells us, or trusting only in the strength and marksmanship of their bare hands. As a rule, they fought almost naked, and those who did not carry a shield used to wrap their left arm in their tamarco to fend off the blows.

10.—THE MENCEY'S CORONATION

The king's proclamation was as follows: the elders of the tribe gathered together in the *Tagoror*, carrying with them a bone wrapped in furs which belonged to the most ancient lineage. They made the proclamation and offered the new king the bone to kiss, after which they placed it on his head and on their own shoulders while chanting: *Agoñe Yacoran Yñatzahaña Chaconamet*. These words meant: «I swear by the bone of that day on which you were exalted». Then, they summoned the people to show them their new sovereign. A public festival followed. This coronation rite was so sacred to them that if it took place in time of war, an inviolable truce was decreed.

11.—Housing

They lived in natural caves or in stone caves with thatched roofs, built when the former were not available. They never constituted a proper nation for their very way of life made this impractical, spending the winter by the sea and the summer in the mountains. At present, there are still many interesting caves in the islands, which were most probably the dwellings of their kings.

Some caves were used as burial places and these were located in inaccessible spots. It is so hard to reach them nowadays that one wonders how they could have carried the mummified corpses there.

12.—Mummification

The most peculiar usage among those primitive people was that of mummifying their dead. Some mummies have withstood the ravages of time due to the utter perfection with which they were preserved.

The only mummies of which there is notice are Egyptian, Peruvian, and Guanche, and this has led many to believe in a common origin for these three people. The Guanches knew well all the secrets of embalming, and their mummies, called *Xaxos*, were treated with a technique similar to that employed in ancient Egypt. According to traditional accounts, there was in the islands, a special caste of men and women who acted as embalmers.

On this topic, Father Espinosa wrote:

«These people were totally ostracized; they had to live in isolation for they were regarded as foul —their only task being to remove the entrails and other decaying portions from the corpses. But, on the other hand, those who specialized in embalming the body were honoured by their fellow citizens...

The dead body was placed on a stone bench and then it

was dissected, its bowels removed. It was washed in cold water mixed with salt twice a day, and special care was taken to soak the ears, nostrils, fingers, toes, and all the most fragile parts. After this, it was anointed with a mixture of goat grease, aromatic herbs, crushed pine bark, resin, fern powder, pumice stone, and other astringents. Then it was exposed to the sun for a forthnight. During this time, the relatives of the deceased sang his praises and mourned. When the body was perfectly mummified, it was wrapped in sheep and goat skins, tanned or raw, according to its rank, and a mark was set upon it in orden to identify it if neccessary. After this ceremony, it was taken to one of the burial caves which were situated in almost inaccessible areas. Those bodies which were buried in sepulchers were arranged against the cave's walls; all the others were laid side by side on some sort of scaffold made of juniper or mocan branches or other non-decaying woods.»

13.—Law

Little is known about the criminal laws in these lands, but it appears that the punishment for offences varied widely from island to island. Manslaughter, for instance, was punished in Tenerife by banishing the guilty from his tribe and depriving him of all his possessions, which were given to the victim's relatives as compensation. In Gran Canaria, however, manslaughter was a light offence. In the island of Hierro, theft was punished by the loss of one eye and that of the other if there was a relapse. In La Palma, however, theft was considered a feat and a proof of courage. As a matter of fact, in Gran Canaria the current penalty in many cases was the *Lex Talionis*, whereas in Tenerife laws were markedly lenient in the punishment of crimes.

The *Tagoror* or Court of Justice assembled in a sort of circus. There were seats for the judges who were chosen among those men who enjoyed the highest reputation. The *Mencey* or chieftain sat on a stone throne covered with furs.

14.—A Whistled Language

The people from Gomera and Hierro communicated by means of a whistled language, especially when the distance was so great that the human vioce could not be audible. This peculiar language was produced by putting one or two fingers of each hand into the mouth in various positions.

It is a characteristic which dates from the most primitive times, and the fact that it is still being used is a proof of the survival of the native race. Is must have been current in Tenerife and in all the other islands, as a natural effect of the environment. The Canarian landscape is extremely rugged with high peaks and deep ravines. It is sometimes neccessary to follow long, steep roads in order to cover short distances. But it is easy to whistle a message from the opposite side of a ravine. Thus it seems obvious that, due to the geopraphical circumstances, the natives perfected this method of whistled communication. Except in places where Semitic migration took place, anthropological research has shown its preservation and continued usage.

The actual language was lost though, when the conquest took place. Nowadays, only proper names and some isolated expressions survive. Towards the end of the nineteenth century, the total number of words compiled amounted to 2,909 —quite a vast vocabulary by all means. Doctor Wölfel's compilation, made in 1940, is presently the most up to date.

XV.— Whistled language, typical among the natives, Island of Gomera.

XVI.—Traditional Chipude pottery, made by the women with extraordinary artistry, Island of Gomera.

CHAPTER V

Cave inscriptions in the Canary Islands and Possible Analogies with other Inscriptions in the American Continent

1.—Rock Carvings

2.—Evidence Pointing to Early Contacts Between the Primitive Inhabitants of the Canary Islands and Those of the American Continent

1.—Rock Carvings

Viera and other writers asserted that the Guanches were skilled in the art of drawing, and the Canarian poet, Viana, spoke about the portrait of the princess Guacimara, «painted on wood with charcoal, ochre, herb juice, and milk from wild fig trees». The poet wrote:

> Ponen los ojos todos al instante
> en la tabla y figura bien pintada
> con tinta de carbón, almagro y zumos
> de varias yerbas y la blanca leche
> de silvestre higuera, y aunque toscos
> los matices, curiosa la hechura,
> y al vivo la figura semejante.

> Soon all are looking / at the wooden panel
> and the lovely portarit, / painted with
> coal ink, red ochre, juices / from various
> herbs, and white milk / from wild fig trees,
> and though the hues / be crude, the shape
> is neat / and the image lifelike.

(VIANA, *Antigüedades de las Islas Afortunadas*, Song III)

It seems only natural that if they knew how to draw and paint, they must have also known how to write.

But the enigma posed by the undeciphered cave inscriptions in the island of Hierro (Los Letreros and Candia), in La Palma (Belmaco and La Zarza), in Tenerife (Anaga), in Gran Canaria (Barranco de Balos), and other islands, has not yet been unveiled.

The inscriptions in *Los Letreres* were first studied in 1870 by Father Aquilino Padron. These *petroglyphs* stand in open country, on the southern part of the island. Padron saw and copied the mysterious inscriptions carved on an old bed of extremely porous basaltic lava, more than 400 meters in length.

Several groupings of totally unknown *petroglyphs* and oddly shaped characters may be seen. Father Padrón, on noting this, wrote: «At first, I took them for Egyptian hieroglyphs, but I looked in vain for human representations, figures seated and mitered; the ox god Apis; the sacred Ibis, that covered the obelisks; and all the other signs typical of this ancient civilization. The only things I saw were the fish and quadrupeds which appear in the old Inca and Mexican calendars.»

But these inscriptions were not only to be found in the island of Hierro. A momentous discovery was to favour the research of this indefatigable priest. Towards the end of 1875, new *petroglyphs* were discovered. In the northern part of the island, in the Candia ravine to the east of Valverde, petroglyphs had been traced on huge leaves stuck together. There they have remained for many years upon the rocks where the inscriptions are.

It has been possible to obtain a fairly exact facsimile, offering an extremely accurate reproduction of these *petroglyphs*: «Here we have a veritable piece of writing, probably narrating a legend commemorating some important event. As far as I am concerned, I think many of the signs in this legend are identical with those found in *Los Letreres*. Moreover, I believe there is a marked similarity between some of these inscriptions and those of Hebrew, Phoenician, and Carthaginian origin, but there are also a series of odd, unknown signs. In short, I am bewildered at all these differences, all these novelties.»

Concerning the *Belmaco petroglyphs* (Island of La Palma), Doctor Carlos de Fritsch of Frankfurt University published in 1862, in Germany, the results of his scientific research in the Canary Islands. In his book can be found, together with some letters, an exact reproduction of several strange signs which he found engraved on a rock in the *Belmaco* cave.

There are fifteen signs in this lapidary inscription, totally identical with those found in Hierro, in the *Los Letreras* cave. Almost all the others are highly similar, as it is easily perceived that the writing is the same —formed by rough arabesques, each word being marked by a particular figure.

In writing about his discovery, Doctor Fritsch said:

«I visited a number of interesting caves, *Belmaco* among them, which is now used to keep oxen. Old Spanish authors had already written about it. Two huge basaltic rocks stand on its entrance; on their flat surfaces, there are some peculiar characters engraved, resembling arabesques and spirals, like hieroglyphs, three or four millimeters in depht and one or two centimeters long, which could only have been engraved with the help of some metallic implement.»

This similarity between the *Belmaco petroglyphs* and those of *Los Letreras* is further proof of the common origin shared by the old islanders. The tribes who lived in the Fortunate Islands were for a very long time in the utmost isolation, for they did not know the art of sailing.

The Inscriptions of Anaga (Tenerife) were studied by Ossna and Van Den-Heede, who wrote *Las Inscripciones de Anaga* describing a series of engraved stones of the third or second century B. C.

«This discovery seems to refute the assertions made by Sedeño, Gómez Escudero, Espinosa, Mesa y Benítez, Abreu Galindo, Viera, Bethelot, Millares, and other historians who maintained that the ancient Guanches did not know how to represent their ideas graphically, whether by the drawing of hieroglyphs or the written word.»

Jiménez Sánchez, when speaking about the inscriptions and rock carvings of *Barranco de Balos,* in the district of Agüimes (Gran Canaria), said that:

«The rock carvings and alphabetic inscriptions found in Barranco de Balos and Los Letreros are part of the most overwhelmingly novel chapter in the prehistory of Gran Canaria, and because of this very novelty, they pose a series of enigmas no one has yet been able to decipher. Those specialists who have studied them, have only been able to offer conjectures as to the people who traced them; or the civilizations to which they belong. Among the theories presented we have one that seees in them a late neolithic manifestation, dating them chronologically between 4,000 and 2,000 before Christ. Another thinks them to be the product of the survival of some people coming from the Near East —especially Phoenicia and Crete— who arrived in the Canary Islands at the end of their long migration. Yet, others see them as examples of the earliest Phoenicia-Cananaean and Cypro-Cretan cultures; or as proto-Guanches from the Cro-Magnon period. There are even those who, like Doctor Wölfel, have pointed out the similarity between them and Norse megalithic carvings, especially in their representation of ships, which he says are almost identical to those of Hällristninger in Northern Scandinavia. Countess Weissen-Szulanka, on the other hand, has come to the conclusion that the Canary Islands were the origin of the ancient Egyptian civilizations, and not the last offshoot of these. She believes that the Canaries were the focal point of Cro-Magnon settlement and dispersion to other lands. Moreover, one can still locate living remains of these people.»

Throughout this chapter, we have been giving the name *petroglyphs* to the signs in the cave inscriptions found in the Canaries. We have not called them hieroglyphs, the usual term employed by other authors to refer to them, because we think that *petroglyph* (from the Greek *petra* meaning rock, and *glyphein*, to carve) is a more accurate name in this case. The kind of writing to which they belong is still totally unknown to us, so that they remain undecipherable. We have regarded them until present simply as signs carved on rocks.

Hieroglyph (from the Greek *hierós*, meaning holy and *glyphein*, to carve) designates, on the other hand, those signs belonging to a known writing system. First deciphered by Champollion, they usually have a sacred character and are carved or painted on rock. We, however, cannot give this name to the inscriptions in the Canary Islands, as we do not know whether they belong to a system of writing or not.

2.—Evidence Pointing to Early Contacts Between the Primitive Inhabitants of the Canary Islands and those of the American Continent

In the light of many recent and earlier discoveries, it seems now highly probable that the ancient and warlike race who came from the North, conquering Egypt and Libya, invading Spain, and leaving traces everywhere of their passage —marking the stages on their way by lapidary inscriptions, barrows, cromlechs, and other similar monuments— could well have reached lands more distant than the Canaries.

History sheds no light on this matter; thus we will avoid offering our conjectures about the possible date of their arrival, for whatever we venture to say about it might give rise to many unanswerable questions. A similar problem is posed by the hypothesis that concerns the seafaring Phoenicians, who acted as mediators among the primitive inhabitants of the Fortunate Islands when, at some unknown date, the migrations to America took place.

Paul Gaffarel, Professor of History at the Dijon Faculty of Letters, published a book in 1875 where he attempted to reveal the traces that proved the relations that existed between the Phoenicians and the Americans. He took the Canary Islands (colonized by the Phoenicians) as one of his starting points and wrote: «Had we not this proof of Phoenician settlement in the Fortunate Islands, we would have had to abandon our thesis, but we think the agreement shown by all ancient traditions and the una imity of geographical accounts have helped us to establish beyond doubt the fact that the Phoenicians knew and probably colonized this archipelago.»

One fact about which we may be certain of, is that there had existed a relation in ancient times between the people of Canarian origin and the inhabitants of America —there are more than thirty words of Caribbean origin found among the proper and place names in the old Guanche tongue.

A new discovery, made in 1839 by the North American Eugene Veil, further substantiated this theory. Mr. Veil found in Grave-Creek, Ohio, a huge barrow where an inscription was carved over three parallel and horizontal lines on one of the stones. These signs were clearly similar to those found in the lapidary inscriptions of the island of Hierro. On this subject, Mr. Jomard has written: «If it is true, as Mr. Berthelot has proved, that there is a striking similitude between some Caribbean words and certain place names and proper names in the old Guanche language; if, furthermore, it was physically impossible that the trade-winds did not, at one time or another, take the natives of the Canary Islands to the opposite shores, then why must we be surprised to find in America traces of their passage? History, no doubt, remains silent about these matters. But we need to give a plausible explanation for the similarity between the rock carvings found in the island of Hierro and those found in an American monument which dates from very ancient times...»

Another fact which deserves attention is that in the Grave-Creek barrow, there was a good number of terracotta grains, highly resembling those which were also found in the burial caves of the Canary Islands.

Conclusive proof in favour of this thesis is the settlement in the northern part of America of the people who carved the lapidary inscriptions of the Canaries. Mr. Simonin, a French scholar and explorer, on his return in 1874 from his fifth voyage to North America, offered the Paris Geographic Society an account of his latest discoveries in the copper mines of Lake Superior, which he visited and which bore traces of having been explored in very ancient times. From this he presumed the existence of a people who lived there before the Redskins. His interest was further awakened when, back in France, he read the report published in the journal of the already mentioned Geographic Society about the Canarian inscriptions. He soon realized there was an odd identity between these strange characters and those on the rocks he himself discovered in America. Thus he commented: «This similitude has been a veritable revelation for me —the same concentric circles in these mysterious signs, resembling coiled serpents; the same round or square shapes.»

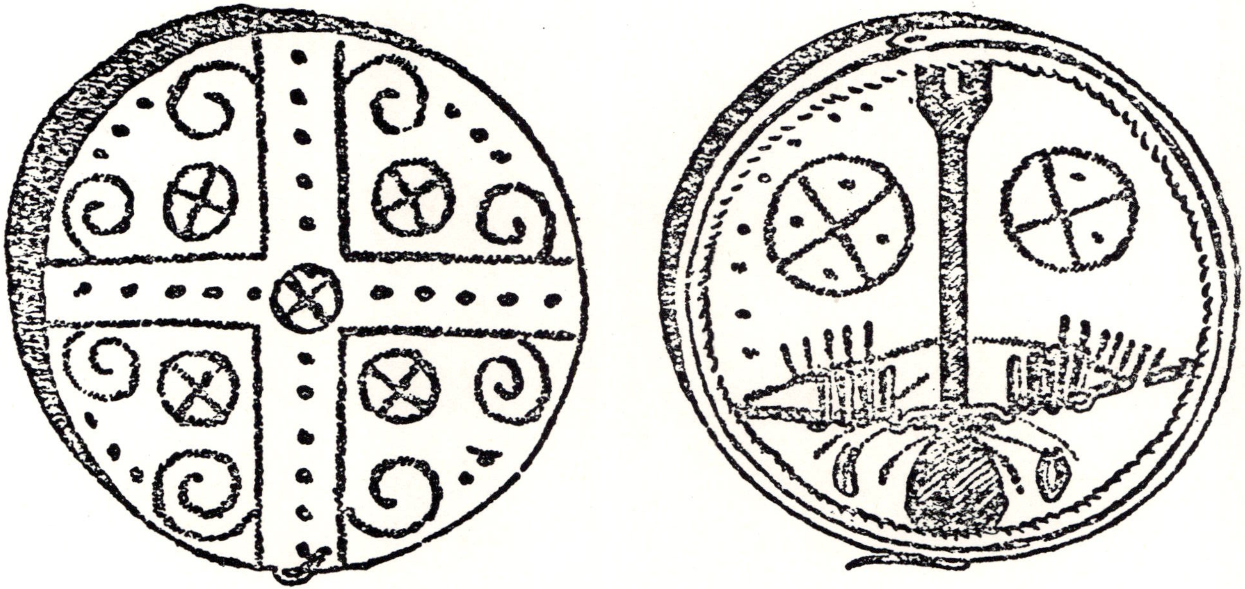

XVII.—The Schaman drum, according to Hermann Wirth in: Die Heilige Urschheit.

XVIII.—Signs assembled in a way which suggest they may form words, found in the inscriptions in Hierro.

XIX.—Petroglyphs carved on the rocks, at the entrance to the Belmaco cave, La Palma, Canary Island.

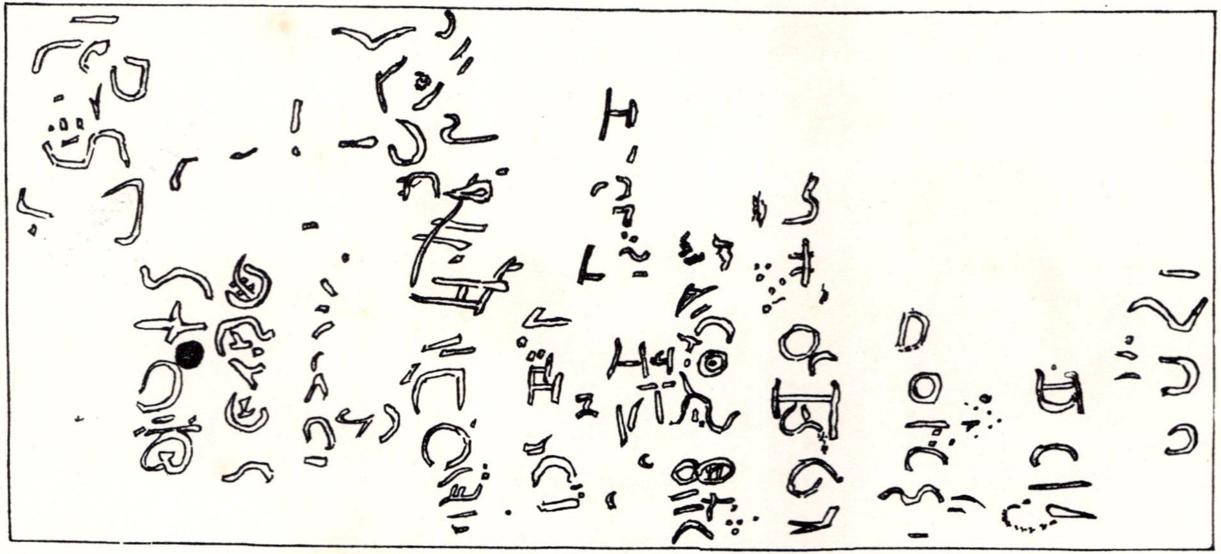

XX.—Inscriptions from the Candia ravine (Hierro), Canary Islands.

A photograph of the places where this discovery was made helped Mr. Simonin to compare the American inscriptions and those of Hierro and La Palma. The identity between these inscriptions proved, beyond doubt, that the people who carved them on the volcanic rocks of the Fortunate Islands were the same ones who left similar carvings on the porphyries of Arizona and California.

Mr. Simoin visited a burial cave on the shores of Salt Lake, from where he took human skulls which, on his return to France, he donated to the Paris Museum of Natural History. Two professors from the National Museum, Messrs. Lartet and Quatrefages, together with Messrs. Pruner, Broca, and Dally, members of the Anthropological Society, compared these skulls with those of the early inhabitants of the Canaries. The five scholars were unanimous in their opinions: there was a perfect correspondence between the characteristics shown by the Canarian craniums and those of the two brought by Mr. Simonin.

Thus, both North America and the old Fortunate Islands were inhabited in remotest antiquity by people having a common origin and belonging to the same race. In America, these people attained a higher degree of civilization. They worked in the mines, were skilful potters and, though not being primarily hunters, shepherds, and warriors like the Guanches, they tilled the soil, reaped, and ground the grain in the same manner.

German Wirth, basing his method of research in the paleoepigraphic system in his book *Die Heilige Urschheit* (1931) or *Early Sacred Writings in the History of Mankind*, showed the marked similarities between the cave paintings of the Old and New Worlds and that this resemblance and the combination of signs were but the calendar on both sides of the Atlantic.

We may take, as an example, an Atlantic symbol written $\substack{\circ \\ \bullet}$ which expresses the idea of the lineal junction between the highest and lowest position of the sun during the year. This sign, according to the cult symbolism of the North American Indians as it reached us in the first half of the nineteenth century, had the meaning of «coming from above and below, life and death, etc....» It turned out to be a general Atlantic symbol signifying «usage and evolution», from which developed the sense of «the sons, the descendants». This ancient ideograph was later substituted by the more modern Atlantic symbol ⚨, a variant at first of the sign ∩. Later on, both the signs ⚮ and ⚨ were linked together in such a way that one of the signs was used as a clarification of the other. This almost mathematical combination was to be found in the prehistory of both the Old and the New Worlds. The same happened with the linking of the sign ⚮ with the symbol for «man» ⵗ. The process was repeated in many other instances.

Wirth pointed out that the cult symbolism of the North American Indians and the Atlantic signs were undoubtedly the same, and presented identical groupings; but this concordance was interrupted when Atlantis disappeared, and from then onwards, these graphic signs suffered different evolutions in the two continents. Further research and more profound studies will one day, perhaps, shed more light on the history of these symbols: «The past will always illuminate the present and offer invaluable lessons for the future.»

CHAPTER VI

Prelude to the Conquest of the Archipelago

1.—Expeditions which Preceded the Conquest of the Canary Islands

2.—Don Luis de la Cerda, Príncipe de la Fortuna

3.—Other Expeditions to the Archipelago

1.—EXPEDITIONS WHICH PRECEDED THE CONQUEST OF THE CANARIES

The fall of the Western Roman Empire was sufficient cause to make Europe forget the Canary Islands. They were busy enough with the terrible barbarian invasions, and could spare neither time nor energies for new adventures.

The Spanish Christians did not mention the Canaries at all during the first gory stages of their fight against the Moors. Their vital concern was to reconquer their native soil, and they cared little about the exploration of new lands. The Arabs, on the other hand, who had come to know the Canaries through Greek works, wrote about them more than once. They gave the name Aldjeriz al-Khalidah, meaning Fortunate Islands, to the Canaries.

In the midst of the utter obscurity that envelops the history of the Canaries for thirteen centuries, an important event has come to light: the establishment of Arab population in Gran Canaria from 999 A. D. onwards.

An Arab captain, Ben-Farroukh, on duty off the Portuguese coasts against possible Norman attacks, got news of the existence of some extraordinarily beautiful islands which lay in the Lybian area. He set sail towards those islands, so vividly described to him, and shortly arrived at Gran Canaria. His account of the voyage was summarized and translated from the Arab original by Mr. Etienne in 1844 and was later published by Mr. Manuel de Ossuna.

Ben-Farroukh, leading 130 men, landed at Gando, a small harbour which owes its name to Arab geographers. He traversed the island from south to north, in a constant struggle with that virgin and exuberant soil which was protected against invaders by woods and deep ravines. He finally arrived at the plains of Galdar, where the *Guanarteme* Guanariga lived. There, the newcomers were welcomed by the prince and his *guayres* (cunsellors). Ben-Farroukh announced to this prince that a powerful monarch desired to enter into an alliance with him. Thus started a friendly relation, highly advantageous for the Arabs, who obtained a secure shelter against piratical attacks for their ships.

The Arabs were entertained by Guanariga in his own palace. There they were offered the most exquisite delicacies Ben-Farroukh and his men had ever eaten. After visiting all the other islands, he returned to Lisbon highly praising the Gran Canaria natives, saying that they were an eminently civilized and hospitable people who enjoyed an advanced social system and that their country flourished in agriculture and in other primitive industries.

Xerif-el-Edrisi, better known as the Nubian geographer, also gave an account of the travels undertaken in the eleventh century by some Arab adventurers, who set out from Lisbon, in his book *The One Desirous to Travel the Earth*. Webb and Berthelot dwelt further on the subject, asserting that, after Pliny's, there was no record mentioning the Fortunate Islands other than the account left by the Maghruin Arabs, who came from Lisbon at the beginning of the twelfth century or perhaps even at an earlier date as Edrisi, who spoke about it in his geography, did not refer to it as a recent event. Edrisi wrote: «It was from Lisbon that these seamen set sail, in the desire to know what the ocean enclosed and which were its limits.»

A series of voyages ensued until the Canarian archipelago was finally conquered. These voyages brought further notice of these islands and awakened in the European nations which fought for supremacy, a desire to possess them.

We will first speak about the Genoese expedition which took place in 1291. Several writers, among them Agustin Giustiniani, recounted how two galleys under the command of Theodosius Doria and Hugolino da Vivaldo were furnished for this voyage. Their purpose was to explore the seas, but they were lost off the western coast of Africa; and though there was no conclusive proof of their having landed at the

Canaries, the fact that they sailed near the Canarian seabord makes it very likely. The etymology of *Lanzarote* may be taken as evidence of a Genoese visit to the Canary Islands. Lanciloto, a nobleman, gave his name to one of the eastern islands.

A far more important expedition was the one sent to the Canary Islands by King Alfonso IV of Portugal. Three caravels, amply supplied with arms and victuals, integrated this expedition. They were manned by Portuguese, Italian, and Spanish sailors, under the leadership of the Florentine *Angiolino del Tegghia de Corbizz*. They left Lisbon on July 1, 1341, and after five days of navigation, they discovered and island 140 miles in circumference (according to the account given by the Genoese navigator, Nicoloso da Recco) where they saw many men and women of a savage appearance and manners, and where they obtained a great quantity of goat skins, tallow, fish oil, seal remains, red birch, and tree bark for dyeing. But they did not dare to venture further inland, as they feared the ferocity of the natives.

Then they went to another, bigger island, the inhabitants of which came to the beach almost naked, though some of them wore a kind of leather apron (saffron or red in colour) which no doubt was a mark of superior dignity. They spoke a language the seamen were unable to understand, but which struck them as being melodious and lively. Their gestures and demeanour showed that they wanted to have intercourse with the foreigners. But as they did not venture to leave their ships, some of the natives swam towards them and were well received on board. These young natives had splendid bodies, long fair hair, and strong limbs. All of them were beardless. Their only garment consisted of a short skirt made of rush or palm leaves. They gave signs of a notable intelligence and vivacity and managed to make themselves understood by means of dumb show. They even explained that their homeland was called Canaria, for that was the island that the expeditioners sent by Alfonso IV had arrived at.

Wanting to pursue their discoveries further, they coasted the island following a northern route, noticing as they progressed in that direction signs of a better soil cultivation and greater activity among the natives. Many houses could be seen, lands were planted with vegetables or covered by gardens where fig, palm and various other trees grew. Encouraged by such a pleasant sight, they decided to put ashore twenty five armed men.

Most of the dwellings were closed, for the frightened islanders had sought the protection of the mountains, and only by loud angry cries did they show their antagonism towards the invaders. The newcomers visited those houses and were charmed by the impeccable neatness of the wooden or stone buildings. They also came across dried figs, preserved in palm baskets and a variety of wheat which far exceeded the quality of the one known in Europe. They also found a stone statuette —the figurine holding a ball in one hand, and its private parts covered. They brought this back to Lisbon.

Laden with booty, they embarked and set sail towards new discoveries. The first of these was the island of Hierro —we presume— because of the rich variety of luxuriant trees described in their memoirs. From there, they went to another island, which must have been La Gomera, because of its proximity to Hierro. Here, those seamen were marvelled by the great number of streams and by the deliciously tasting pigeons, which fed on laurel berries, and cherries. After sighting La Palma, with its high and cloudy peaks, they saw before them a land of magic, where an amazing prodigy filled them with awe: a huge mount crowned with some white substance which constantly changed shapes. These marvellous arabesques persuaded the superstitious sailors that a hellish spirit lived there. But such a puzzling marvel, such a mysterious land was none other than the island of Tenerife and the proud peak of the Teide.

They counted up to thirteen islands: the total number of islands in the archipelago if one adds the less known Lobos, Roque del Este, Roque del Oeste, Graciosa, Montaña Clara, and Alegranza to Gran Canaria, Tenerife, La Palma, Gomera, Hierro, and Fuerteventura.

This expedition opened new and vast horizons. To it we

owe the first accurate account of the geographical situation of the Canary Islands. Forgotten until then, or incorrectly placed on the maps, now they found their proper place. To it indeed did Europe owe the most exact and faithful notice about a land whose existence had been so problematic and enveloped in the mists of legend and myth. This expedition also proved that in the midst of the unknown western seas, there lived other civilized people who knew about agriculture, industry, architecture, and art. Moreover, the distinctions they observed concerning dress, house construction and care, and certain manifestations of respect shown to some individuals, hinted at a well established social order.

The spirit of pilgrimage and conquest, which increased daily, soon drew the most daring adventurers to this new land —men who now turned longing eyes towards the West which, to their inflamed imaginations, seemed a fruitful field where richess and glory could be won. Powerful monarchs were also attracted by these lands and strove to make them theirs.

2.—Don Luis de la Cerda, Príncipe de la Fortuna

No other prince was so intent in conquering the Canaries as the infante Don Luis de la Cerda, Count of Clermont, who belonged to the disinherited branch of Castile and had been brought up at the courts of Aragón and France.

The difficult situation in which the boundless ambition of Sancho II had placed the *infantes*, direct descendants of the Wise King, Alfonso X, incited Don Luis to seek the protection of Pope Clement VI, and beg from him the crown of the Canaries.

Viera y Clavijo tells us that the Pope held a public consistory, where the Canaries were proclaimed a kingdom, though the original bulls asserted that the islands were declared a principality and as such were given to Don Luis de España, a name by which he was also known. He was then proclaimed feudatory of the Apostolic See and had to pay the Roman Church a tithe of 400 gold floring *of the best and purest quality, of Florentine weight and coinnage.* The bull was drawn up in Avignon on the fitteenth of November, 1344, and the solemn investiture took place towards the end of December, in that very same city.

Alfonso XI, King of Spain, wrote a letter dated May 13, 1345, in Alcalá de Henares, protesting against this proclamation, as he maintained that the Canary Islands belonged to the Moroccan diocese, suffragan to the diocese of Seville. The King of Portugal also aired his protest before the Pope, for he believed that the expeditions he had already sent and the preparations he had made to conquer the islands —a feat he could not accomplish because of his wars against the King of Castile and the Moorish princes— had given him a right over the Canaries.

3.—OTHER EXPEDITIONS TO THE ARCHIPELAGO

But more voyages to the Canaries were to take place before the final conquest. The most important ports in Europe saw a continuous flow of armed fleets, which set sail in quest of booty and plunder, under the disguise of bringing to that promised land the magnificent boon of the True Faith.

In 1360, two galleys manned by Mallorquines and Aragoneses landed at *Gando*. Venturing too far inland without securing a safe retreat, they and five Franciscan friars accompanying them were all captured. As a turn of fate, the captives earned the friendship of their captors because of the many useful things they taught them, such as the planting of fig trees and the building of comfortable houses. This happy state of affairs, however, deteriorated as years went by. The islanders, unwilling to submit sometimes to demands that went against their code of honour, were forced to take severe measures and condemned their captives to death. According to tradition, the five friars were thrown over the cliff of Jinamar, the punishment meted out to traitors and adulterers.

Another attempt, bearing less tragic results, took place in 1377. The Biscayan captain, Martín Ruiz de Avendaño, a member of the Royal Navy, was cast ashore by a storm and had to remain for some time in Lanzarote, living in perfect harmony with the natives.

A Galician nobleman, Don Fernando de Ormel, Count of Ureña, suffered a similar misfortune and landed at Gomera, where the Europeans, who attacked the natives, were taken prisoners. They were later released and allowed to go on board their caravel.

The most important expedition during those years was the one sent in 1392 or 1399 by a partnership of Andalusian, Biscayan, and Guipuzcoan shipowners. They sailed from Seville and plundered Lanzarote, although they did not dare attack Tenerife for they had been badly frightened by one of the Teide's eruptions. These repeated attempts foreshadowed the great conquest of the Canary Islands.

There is one more thing worthy of notice: the humane behaviour of the islanders, who showed loftier feelings than those that animated the Europeans. In granting life and freedom to their enemies, they clearly evince the superiority of that handsome, courageous and noble race.

CHAPTER VII

The Conquest of the Canaries under the Patronage of the Crown of Castile

1.—Aspects of the Conquest
2.—A Warlike Race
3.—Juan de Bethencourt, First Conqueror of the Canaries
4.—Brief Account of Bethencourt's Expedition to Lanzarote and Fuerteventura
5.—Bethencourt Pays Homage to the King of Castile in the Name of the Canary Islands
6.—Berthin de Berneval's Rebellion
7.—Atchen's Treason. The Outbreak of War
8.—Gadifer's Visit to the Canarian Archipelago
9.—Bethencourt's Return and the Surrender of Lanzarote
10.—Second Expedition to Fuerteventura and an Account of Some of the Events Which Took Place There
11.—Dangerous Disagreements Between the Two Commanders of the Expedition
12.—Fuerteventura's Surrender
13.—Bethencourt's Third Voyage to Europe
14.—Bethencourt's Return to the Canary Islands
15.—Bethencourt's Visit to the African Coast and the Canarian Archipelago
16.—The Conquest of the Island of Hierro
17.—Bethencourt's Return to his Native Country
18.—Death of Bethencourt

1.—Aspects of the Conquest

The expeditions so far reviewed in the preceding chapters (III and VI) must be taken as mere voyages of exploration. But Juan de Bethencourt's enterprise actually constitutes the starting point of the conquest. It was then that a foreign power really established itself in the Canary Islands.

The conquest of the archipelago lasted from 1402 until 1496 and was marked by two different stages. The first stage opens with Juan de Bethencourt's voyage, under the auspices of the Crown of Castile, the sovereignty of which was accepted by the Norman nobleman, who made its name prevail in all his negotiations at Court, as an act of vassalage. During this period, and under the patronage of Henry III of Castile, some of the Canary Islands were annexed to Spain (Hierro, Fuerteventura, and Lanzarote). The claims of Spain over the archipelago had already been recognized since the days of Alphonso XI.

The second stage starts about half a century later, when the Catholic King and Queen, while accepting the rights granted by royal letters patent to the Lords of Lanzarote, take over the conquest of the island, which is now regarded as a national enterprise. As such it is pursued, as a noble and generous quest, in the desire to bring civilization and Christianity to those unlettered and heathen people.

The Crown then assumed direct responsibility for the endeavour and if captains sometimes deviated from those high ideals, they were, on the main, faithful to the noble aims of the monarchs.

The long interval of years in between the two stages showed no progress in the conquest and, sometimes, relations between the islanders and the Europeans, or even among the Europeans

103

themselves, degenerated to such an extent that the efforts of the first conquerors seemed to have been in vain.

During this period, the Crown encouraged private attempts to conquer the islands, but many of the adventurers were activated only by ambition and cupidity, so that injustice and extortion often prevailed in spite of the Crown's efforts to curtail these evils.

Ferdinand and Isabella established a lawful regime in the archipelago, under which the natives mixed with the conquerors, thus forming a united nation, firmly bound to their mother country.

2.—A Warlike Race

The Spaniards soon realized how sturdy, bold, courageous to the point of temerity, and warlike their enemies were. Capable of the cruellest reprisals when attacked but, on the other hand, generous and humane if not provoked, this race, as historians would testify, demonstrated an interesting mixture of human qualities. They were unlettered, but they possessed the highest spiritual values.

The Peruvian and Mexican Indians, defeated even before the fight began, opposed a weak resistance to their invaders. Their lords' and priests' slaves, through weakness and indolence brought about the fall of two empires, which were already undermined by tyranny and superstition. But the Canarian islanders were of quite a different mettle; the mere thought of slavery repelled these people, who were infinitely proud of their rights. The Mexican thought the Spaniards were gods, but the Guanches saw them as men and, as such, found much to despise in their behaviour.

3.—Juan de Bethencourt, First Conqueror of the Canaries

The primary stage in the conquest of the Canaries began with the expedition of Juan de Bethencourt, Baron of St. Martin of Gaillard, in the country of Eu in Normandy. This Norman knight belonged to a noble family and had won distinction both at war and at sea. He was appointed chamber-

XXI.—The prehistoric cave of Belmaco, at Mazo, Island of La Palma, with rock carvings.

XXII.—Prehistoric cave of la Zarza, Garafía, Island of La Palma, with rock carvings.

XXIII.—Juan de Bethencourt, first conqueror of the Canaries.

XXIV.—The Conquest's Cross, at the parish church of La Concepción, Santa Cruz de Tenerife.

lain under Charles VI; but, weary of Court services during the King's insanity, and unhappy in his private life, he left his palace of Grainville la Teinturiere, in Caux, and resolved to win fame and glory by means of some exploit. He was soon to find his chance: the Canaries.

Towards 1393, a Spanish nobleman surnamed Almonaster (father of Fernán Peraza, husband of Doña Inés de las Casas) landed at Lanzarote and brought back with him a number of prisioners and some products, which testified to the great fertility of the Canarian archipelago. Bethencourt was greatly impressed by this adventure and, wishing to enlarge his fortune and earn high renown, he set his heart upon conquering the Canary Islands. With this aim in mind, he surrounded himself with influential people: the Franciscan Fray Pedro Bontier, Father Juan Le Verrier, who were to be Bethencourt's chaplains and the expedition's chroniclers, and many others. Among his followers we also find two Canarian captives who had been baptized and given the names of Alfonso and Isabel. They proved to be valuable as interpreters later on.

The expedition arrived first at La Rochelle, and there the knight Gadifer de la Salle (the Don Gaiferos of the ballads) and several other adventurers embarked too. Their ship left La Rochelle on May 1, 1402, arriving at Vivero and then at Corunna and Cadiz, where they remained for some days. The company soon diminished through the desertion of twenty six men, so Bethencourt was left with only fifty three followers.

In the month of July, eight days after leaving Cadiz, they discovered three desert islands in succession, which they named Alegranza, Montaña Clara, and Graciosa. Bethencourt and his company did not stop but continued his chartered course until a vast coastline appeared in the horizon. This was none other than the island of Lanzarote.

Ancient traditions say that this land had been divided into two different states. This partition must have taken place in a very distant past, as the island had already been united under one monarch many years before the conquest. Around 1377, the king of Lanzarote was one Zonzamas. It was then that a violent gale cast ashore one of the ships commanded by the Biscayan nobleman Martin Ruiz de Avendaño. The company was so well received and entertained by the natives that Avendaño remained in the island for some time. Zonzamas courteously offered him his own palace and even his extremely beautiful queen, Fayna, a most striking gift. The grateful Avendaño eagerly accepted such an offering and made her pregnant, so that in due time Fayna was delivered of a baby girl who was called Ico.

Shortly afterwards, Tiguafaya, the son of Zonzamas, became king. The Spaniards invaded the island and defeated the natives, capturing many prisoners, including the monarchs, and brought them, together with a rich booty, to Spain. Because of this the crown passed to Guanarteme, who married the fair Ico. His reign was short and hazardous; his son Guardafía succeeded him.

In spite of so many calamities, the islanders had not forgotten Ico's illegitimacy, and she had always been regarded as a foreigner. So, they required her to prove her noble origin by means of the «smoke test», and unless she submitted to it, they refused to acknowledge Guardafía's rights to the throne. This harrowing test consisted in locking the unfortunate queen and three other women in a room filled with smoke. If she, like the other three commoners, died, then her base origin was proved.

Ico, forced to endure such an ordeal, equipped herself with a big sponge soaked in water and thanks to this trick, which an old woman had revealed to her, she was able to avoid suffocation. Thus, Ico managed to secure the throne for her son.

4.—Brief Account of Bethencourt's Expedition to Lanzarote and Fuerteventura

Bethencourt unsuccessfully attempted a reconnoitering of Lanzarote. After his first failure, he retreated to the islet of Alegranza, where he held a council of war and decided to return to Lanzarote with all his men.

No sooner had Bethencourt landed than a crowd of islanders approached in welcome, showing him every sign of respect and consideration. One of them, who was wearing the old goat-skin-and-shells crown, which was distinctive of the kings of the island, urgently begged him to protect them against the plundering and pillaging of pirates. In return, he offered the Spaniard his friendship and promised his submission «as friend, not as subject».

Bethencourt was encouraged by such a heartening reception. He had the castle of Rubicon built in the southeast area of the island, and appointed Berthin de Berneval as its commander. He then set sail for the island of Fuerteventura, but food ahortage and the ill will of his companions doomed the enterprise. Bethencourt had to return to Lanzarote, where his people had mutinied, and then he was forced to return to Spain to revictual in order to resume the adventure. He appointed his lieutenant, Gadifer de la Salle, governor of Lanzarote in his absence.

5.—Bethencourt Pays Homage to the King of Castile in the Name of the Canary Islands

When Bethencourt disembarked at Cadiz, he learned that the Court was in Seville. He journeyed there to swear allegiance to the King of Castile in the name of the Canaries. Henry graciously welcomed Bethencourt, who enjoyed the patronage of his uncle, Roberto de Braquemont, a very influential man at court.

The Spanish monarch bestowed upon Bethencourt the government of all the islands which had not yet been conquered; the right to have his own coinage; one-fifth over exports; 20,000 maravedís to pay the expenses of a second voyage; and a ship well-furnished and heavily armed, which was sent to Gadifer.

This could well be regarded as the true beginning of the conquest, one of the most glorious feats ever accomplished by the Crown of Castile. Had it not been for the practical help of Henry III, Bethencourt would have faced insurmountable difficulties. Though it is true that the powerful Catholic monarchs did exert the greatest influence on the conquest, as we will see later on.

While Bethencourt remained in Spain, taking the necessary measures to secure the success of his enterprise, several important changes were occurring in the Canaries. (A brief account of them will be made, as a detailed account will not be possible due to spacial limitations.)

6.—BERTHIN DE BERNEVAL'S REBELLION

Berneval, commander of the Rubicón castle and sworn enemy of Gadifer, availed himself of the latter's departure for the island of Lobos in search of seal skins, which they needed for their footwear, and revolted. At the head of a group of rebels he captured by suprise the king of Lanzarote and twenty three of his noblemen, putting them on board the Spanish ship *Tajamar*. Guardafía, however, managed to escape.

In addition, Berneval ordered his men to seize the ship Gadifer sent from Lobos under the command of Remmonet de Leveden. The ship was to procure fresh victuals for the expeditioners. Remmonet tried to put up a fight, but he and his men were outnumbered. They were unable to prevent Berneval and his men from pillaging and destroying the supplies, tools, and weapons Juan de Bethencourt had stored in the castle of Rubicon.

Meanwhile, Gadifer and his companions were suffering from thirst and hunger and they would have died in the desert inlet of Lobos had it not been for the Spanish Captain Francisco Calvo, who came to their rescue in his ship *Morella*, moved by the ardent pleas of the two chaplains Bontier and Le Verrier. Calvo managed to clear «the most dangerous pass to be found this side of the ocean» and brought aid to the noble Gadifer, who was already at the end of his endurance.

Berneval's treason was not complete yet. He not only betrayed his lord but also those who helped him to perpetrate his crimes. He put ashore twelve of them and set sail towards Spain, where he intended to secure Bethencourt's approval for what he had done, by making up a convincing story. As he did not want to have dangerous witnesses around, he abandoned these men to their fate. The poor wretches thought at first to place themselves at the mercy of the governor but, fearing Gadifer's revenge, they stole a ship and fled in a desperate attempt towards the Barbary coast «where twelve of them were drowned and the rest were sold as slaves».

7.—ATCHEN'S TREASON. THE OUTBREAK OF WAR

Many momentous events took place in Lanzarote during this time. King Guardafía, deeply vexed by Bernavel's treason, rose up in arms and with the help of some of his men killed several of Gadifer's companions. Gadifer demanded their instant punishment and one of Guardafía's kinsmen, *Atchen*, offered the Spaniard his help in kidnapping the king and deposing him, after which he himself intended to ascend the throne. But *Atchen* was a thorough villain. After becoming a traitor to his king, he aimed to betray the Normans too. Gadifer, unaware of his true intentions and eager to avenge his friends, accepted *Atchen's* proposal. *Atchen* then informed him that Guardafía had sought refuge in the village of Acatif and had only fifty men with him. Gadifer immediately set out for the village with twenty companions, seized the king, and took him to the castle where he was put in chains.

Shortly afterwards, *Atchen* became the new king of the island and then attacked Gadifer and his men, mortally wounding many of them. But the next night, Guardafía managed to escape and captured *Atchen* and had him stoned and burnt.

The governor of the island, profoundly angered by the violent encounters which took place almost daily, decided to kill all the natives, with the exception of the women and children, whom he intended to have baptized.

8.—GADIFER'S VISIT TO THE CANARIAN ARCHIPELAGO

The ship laden with supplies which Bethencourt had sent to Gadifer finally arrived. This vessel not only brought eighty new men and plenty of victuals, but also a letter from Bethencourt himself, addressed to Gadifer, and informing the latter, among other things, of the allegiance he had sworn to the King of Castile in the name of the Canary Islands. This news deeply upset Gadifer, for he had planned to secure part of those islands for himself. But he masked his dissatisfaction and gave a warm welcome to the newcomers.

Availing himself of the ship and the supplies Bethencourt had sent from Spain, Gadifer sailed towards Fuerteventura and Gran Canaria. He coasted Hierro, arrived at night at Gomera, touched at La Palma, and returned to Rubicón after three months of absence. He managed to trade with the natives of Gran Canaria and took some prisoners from the other islands.

9.—Bethencourt's Return and the Surrender of Lanzarote

Bethencourt arrived at his juncture and was happily greeted by his men. Shortly afterwards, he captured Guardafía and ten of his followers. Realizing that everything was lost, he begged and obtained Bethencourt's mercy; and the people of Lanzarote surrendered on February 27th, 1404.

This is certainly a historical date, as it was then that Guardafía was baptized by Le Verrier. He was christened Luis. The natives soon followed their king's example and were initiated into the Catholic Faith. It was the first and outstanding triumph of Christianity in the ancient lands of Atlantis.

Some historians ascribed the present name of the island to the Genoese Lancelotto, who arrived there in 1312. Others believe that the island owes its name to a French nobleman surnamed Lancelot, who came with Bethencourt.

10.—Second Expedition to Fuerteventura and an Account of Some of the Events Which Took Place There

Bethencourt, true lord of Lanzarote at last, thought the time had come to attempt the conquest of Fuerteventura. He could now count on a numerous expeditionary corps integrated by his brave Spanish and French soldiers, and also by native sappers. So he set sail for a second time towards the dangerous island.

The island was divided into two different and warlike kingdoms, and between them stood a high wall —the remains of which could still be seen until comparatively recent times.

This wall separated the island into two districts: the northern district of *Majorata*, and the southern canton of *Jandía*.

Bethencourt first landed at the coast of *Majorata*, where he took a good number of prisoners who were immediately sent to Lanzarote. But his fears were not appeased when he observed that the natives seemed to be ready to oppose a tenacious resistance. These warlike people attacked from everywhere, blocking all the advances of the invading party. But in spite of so many difficulties, the conquerors managed to erect the fort of *Ricorroque,* so called in memory of the Norman ship *Riche-Roche.* The strategic position of this fort greatly facilitated the progress of the Spaniards in conquering the land.

11.—DANGEROUS DISAGREEMENTS BETWEEN THE TWO COMMANDERS OF THE EXPEDITION

There arose strong differences between Bethencourt and Gadifer until Bethencourt sent an expedition, headed by Gadifer, to Gran Canaria. The company arrived shortly afterwards at the port of Arganyguy, but after a fruitless attempt, Gadifer was forced to return to Fuerteventura. There a ship carrying fresh supplies had recently arrived. It was sent by the King of Castile to Bethencourt and this aroused the jealousy of Gadifer, who from then onwards started to complain of everything. His envy grew day by day; violent quarrels ensued and Gadifer was heard to say more than once that things had not been accomplished thanks to the Baron de Bethencourt alone. These words reached the ears of the Norman nobleman, who was deeply annoyed and upbraided the envious Gadifer.

Gadifer then resolved to leave the Canary Islands where, or so he said, the longer he stayed the lesser he would achieve. At about this time Juan de Bethencourt, after settling his affairs in order, intented to return to Spain. He persuaded Gadifer to accompany him, in order to «settle their differences». Both noblemen arrived at Seville, where Gadifer put his complaints before the king of Castile. But the monarch did not think Gadifer's accusations justified and he totally approved of Bethencourt's behaviour. Consequently, Gadifer left Spain, returning to France, and he never set foot on the Canary Islands again.

The king then gave Bethencourt letters patent which bestowed upon him the domain of the Canaries; and with these, he returned to Fuerteventura.

12.—Fuerteventura's Surrender

Bethencourt was greatly assisted —financially and militarily— in the Fuerteventura enterprise by the King of Castile. The brave islanders offered a tenacious resistance, but Bethencourt was the victor in every encounter. The Norman commander defeated the princes *Guize* and *Ayoze*, two chieftains who ruled the two districts of *Majorata* and *Jandía* respectively.

On January 18, 1408, the king of *Majorata*, with a retinue of forty two men, came to the fort of *Ricorroque* to be baptized. Three days later, the king of *Jandía* and forty seven of his men were likewise baptized in *Valtarahal*, the fort built at the other side of the island. Soon all the natives of Fuerteventura followed suit and the whole island became part of Bethencourt's domain.

This island was given its name —Forte Adventure— by Bethencourt's chaplains. According to Abreu Galindo, *Majorata* was another name given to the island by its ancient inhabitants. The descendants of these are still called *majoreros*.

13.—Bethencourt's Third Voyage to Europe

After achieving such spectacular victories, Bethencourt longed to visit his native country again and thus, on the 31st of January, he handed over his command of Fuerteventura to Juan de Courtois, whom he appointed second in command. He sailed for Europe, taking with him three native men and one woman. He left for «God wanted to take him away and then bring him back again», as the chronicle says. Twenty one days after leaving Fuerteventura, he arrived at the port of Harfleur and, two days afterwards, he was once again in his beautiful manor of *Grainville*.

He was enthusiastically received. Everybody marvelled at his courage. He had achieved a feat which, in those warlike and adventurous days, could not but please his contemporaries, inflamed by a passion for chivalry. But, in the midst of such rejoicings, Bethencourt never forgot that his vast enterprise had only begun. So it happened that even there, and even in those days in which he seemed to be only enjoying a much deserved rest, he managed to further forward his conquest. He vividly described the beauty of the Canaries —the mildness of their climate and their unruffled peace. He tempted his audience by offering to grant them lands and thus awakened in them boundless hopes of glory and adventure. This policy bore its fruits when the time for departure came, for many of Bethencourt's noble friends were ready to follow him. 125 soldiers, the majority of whom brought their families with them, also joined the party. A variegated company, men ready to take part in the adventure without asking for any fixed retribution, enlisted. Among them were the noblemen Juan de Rouillè, Juan de Plessis, Maciot de Bethencourt, and others.

14.—Bethencourt's Return to the Canary Islands

Bethencourt and his men sailed out of Harfleur in two ships on 9 May, 1405. Favourable winds soon took them to the coasts of Lanzarote and Fuerteventura, and they landed at Rubicón beach towards the beginnings of July.

The Norman lord was welcomed to the merry fanfare of trumpets, bugles, and other musical instruments. The natives, rejoicing in their governor's return, danced, sang, and shouted: «Now our king is come!» Juan de Courtois went immediately to pay his respects to Bethencourt, who was naturally anxious to know had things been faring. «My lord —said Courtois— everything is all right and ever improving».

The newcomers were lodged with Bethencourt at the fort of Lanzarote. They were greatly pleased by the country, and enjoyed eating dates and other fruits.

After spending some time in Lanzarote, Juan de Bethencourt sailed for Fuerteventura with his new associates. The welcome they were offered there was no less warm; and the natives, with their two kings, showed them an unsurpassed courtesy and hospitality. The two monarchs dined with the conqueror in the fortress of Ricorroque which Juan de Courtois had repaired. Bethencourt then went to *Valtarahal*, where he intented to supervise the building of a chapel in honour of the Blessed Virgin, dedicating it to *Our Lady of Betancuria*. He had it decorated with an image of Our Lady, a beautiful missal, two small bells (each weighing 100 pounds), and various hangings and ornaments which he had brought from France. Juan de Verrier was chosen parish priest, and he remained in that island until his death —so record the annals of the conquest.

15.—BETHENCOURT'S VISIT TO THE AFRICAN COAST AND THE CANARIAN ARCHIPELAGO

Once the conquest of Lanzarote and Fuerteventura had been achieved, Bethencourt's ambitions were now concentrated on Gran Canaria. The voyages of reconnaissance which had taken place prior to that date had only yielded some trade relations, on which the natives were apparently keen.

The soldiers on which Bethencourt could count were few in number, if the invasion of Gran Canaria was to be considered, as the island was protected by more than 10,000 men. On top of this, Bethencourt had to leave behind part of his small force, for the custody and maintenance of his other dominions. In spite of such setbacks, the brave Norman equipped three galleys and commanded the new expedition. They sailed for Canaria on 6 October, 1405, but a violent gale off the coasts of Africa drove the three galleys ashore, not far from Cape Bojador. Bethencourt and his men left the ships and went inland. They captured some natives and three thousand camels, which they carried to the beach. He put some of these animals on board, for he thought it wise to acclimatize them to the Canaries. Then, they left Cape Bojador which, according to this account, he had discovered thirty years before the Portuguese.

The expedition then continued towards Gran Canaria. But

adverse winds scattered the three galleys: one of them returned to Fuerteventura, the other sought refuge in the island of La Palma, and the third, with Bethencourt on board, was the only one to arrive at Gran Canaria. A few days afterwards it was rejoined by the one which had gone to Fuerteventura.

In spite of Bethencourt's disapproval, the nobleman Guillermo de Auberbose and forty five other men set forth to explore the new land. A pitched battle between Europeans and islanders ensued. The natives lost their king, *Artemi-Semidán*, but the invaders had to mourn the deaths of Auberbose, Godofredo de Anzomuille, and Juan de Courtois, Bethencourt's second in command.

Those who survived this defeat arrived shortly afterwards, under the leadership of Bethencourt, at the island of La Palma. There the third ship awaited them; the crew had not been very successful in their encounters with the natives. The Norman leader spent six days at La Palma, but did not dare to attempt its conquest, in view of the courage shown by the islanders. Instead, he resolved to sail at once towards Hierro.

16.—THE CONQUEST OF THE ISLAND OF HIERRO

The island of Hierro was ruled at that time by a king called *Armiche*. *Augerón*, *Armich's* brother, had been taken prisoner by the Spaniards a few years before, and now was one of the men in Bethencourt's party. He had an interview with his brother, and such was his persuasive force that *Armiche* agreed to meet Bethencourt and discuss a peaceful settlement with him. The Canarian prince trusted Bethencourt and surrendered together with 111 of his men. But the Norman violated every right and took them as prisoners, handing them over to his men as if they were cattle. He retained thirty one for himself, the king among them, and his share of the booty. Bethencourt's chaplains record that some of them were sold as slaves —this having been allowed by the Norman because of two reasons: to satisfy the demands of his confederates, and to have land where some of the families he had brought from Normandy could settle. Thus he left 120 of these families in Hierro and he chose them among those skilled in working the land. But this did not justify in the least his violation of the prince's trust. It is to be lamented that such a deceitful deed besmirched Bethencourt's brilliant career.

This island, called Pluviala or Ombrion in classical times, was christened *Ile de Fer* by Bethencourt. He spent three months there and then sailed to Gomera, arriving at a time when the death of King *Amalahuise* had divided the island into four kingdoms. Such was the passion of the four warring factions that two of the parties those of *Agana* and *Hipalán*, preferred to surrender to Bethencourt rather than surrender to their native enemies. The other two principalities, those of *Mulaga* and *Orone*, preferred to fight the Norman nobleman. These events made the conquest of Gomera one sad story of boodshed and cruelty.

It is interesting to note that neither Juan de Bethencourt nor Maciot, his nephew, were able to conquer Gomera. The natives proved very difficult to overcome and the island did not become part of the Spanish Crow until 1488. It may be said that Gomera became «Spanish» more through contact and trade than through armed intervention. This is highly significant, considering that Gomera is one of the smallest islands in the archipelago. The profound love of freedom shown by the islanders cannot but win our admiration.

Viera y Clavijo, and other historians after him, mistakenly assert that the island of Gomera was conquered by Bethencourt. Bethencourt's chroniclers say nothing about it and this point is further ratified by the account of the Portuguese expedition of 1443. Azurara, the historian in this expedition, categorically stated that La Gomera was still ruled by its native princes and that Maciot had been unable to accomplish the conquest of the island.

The Romans called this island Junonia Minor. Some historians believe its present name derives from that of a French nobleman, Goumier de la Salle, a friend or kinsman of Gadifer, who was governor of the island at one time.

The Baron of Bethencourt returned to Fuerteventura towards the end of 1406, and established his court at *Valtarahal*.

He had then conquered three islands: Lanzarote, Fuerteventura, and Hierro. His domains were so vast that careful consideration had to be given to their spiritual and temporal welfare. Thus, Bethencourt devoted his time to settle his states in order, taking some beneficial and disinterested measures. He became a sort of Canarian king, feudatory to the crown of Spain, and as such, he now proceeded to allot the conquered lands. He exempted his vassals from taxes for nine years, with the sole exception of a third over the fruits of the earth, which would be paid in lieu of church tithes, while religious cult did not need further revenues. He had two churches built and generously distributed his private income. He then appointed Maciot de Bethencourt, his nephew, viceroy or second in command.

After taking such financial measures, he toured the country accompanied by a large retinue, in order to establish his nephew's authority. During this progress, he made it known everywhere that he was soon returning to Europe, so that all those who wanted to place complaints before him should come to his castle at Rubicón before he left. He remained at the castle until December 15, 1406. Once in Lanzarote, and two days prior to his departure, he summoned all those noblemen who had come with him, all his servants, and the three Canarian kings, for he wanted to let them know his will and commend them to God.

Before setting out on his journey, he told his nephew, Maciot: «Moreover, I bestow upon you full power and authority to command and perform whatever you believe useful and honourable, bearing always in mind my honour and profit first. Try to implant as soon as possible Norman and French usages where the law is concerned and in all other things you think fit. I have nothing else to tell you save my urgent entreaty to be at peace among yourselves and, if you do so, everything will be all right.»

17.—BETHENCOURT'S RETURN TO HIS NATIVE COUNTRY

On 13 December a magnificent banquet was held at Rubicón. The three Canarian kings, together with the most important native chieftains, were invited. Once the repast was over, **Bethencourt** mounted a dais and, from there, he once again requested all present to respect and obey his nephew, and pay him a *quinto* (one-fifth) on every product for his own revenues. Two days afterwards, accompanied by his chaplain, **Juan Le Verrier**, his squire, Juan de Bouille, and six other members of his household, he sailed homeward bound.

Nothing better showed the true greatness of this Norman leader than the moving farewell the islanders paid him. The chroniclers described it thus: «Once our Sire had taken his leave of all his people and his country, he put to sea; and everybody burst in tears, uttering heartbreaking cries of sorrow. And what joy for him to hear the saddened natives say: "Why are you leaving us, you, who are our legitimate lord? We will not see you again! Alas! What will become of this unhappy country now that such a wise and judicious lord is gone, he who has shown the way of salvation to so many souls!"»

He arrived at Seville after six days of uneventful voyage. From there he went to Valladolid, where Henry III and his court were. Bethencourt obtained from the King some letters of introduction to the Pope, as he longed to secure a bishopric for the Canary Islands. The King welcomed him warmly and loaded him with presents and then gave him the letters he had requested. After this, the Baron de Bethencourt, taking with him a splendid retinue, sailed for Rome.

He spent three weeks in Rome and was allowed to pay homage to the Pope, Innocent VII, who congratulated him on the conquest and conversion of the Canary Islands. He likewise praised him for the courage he had shown in leaving France for such distant lands. Then the bulls were drawn up and, according to Bethencourt's wishes, Alberto de las Casas was appointed Bishop of the Canaries. Thus the Norman nobleman, after being blessed, took his leave of the Pope and started his journey to France. He visited Florence on his way, where he was given an enthusiastic reception. Once in France he was warmly welcomed too, for if people had flocked to see him when he first arrived there, now, on this second journey, the crowds were even more numerous.

Santiago Rodriguez, however, puts forward a completely different thesis concerning Bethencourt's last voyage. In his notes to the new edition of *Descripción Histórica y Geográfica de las Islas Canarias* by Pedro Agustín del Castillo de Vergara, he writes:

A: Here, there must be a basic inaccuracy, if we accept *Margry's* chronology and the logic course of events; this, moreover, makes it impossible for the following incidents to have happened. It is true that King Henry III stayed at Valladolid from December 21-24, 1406, and Robert de Braquemont, Bethencourt's uncle, was there on these dates too, having undertaken such journey, together with the Bishop of Saint-Flour, in order to conclude a treaty on behalf of the King of France. But on December 25, 1406, King Henry III died, and thus, all that is narrated here sounds highly unlikely, as such events clearly could not have taken place; nor was it possible for Bethencourt to have seen the King. According to *Margry*, he left the Canaries on December 15, 1406 and it took him six days to arrive at Seville (the twenty-second), where he remained until the twenty-sixth. The French manuscript says that the King received him and that Bethencourt was detained at Valladolid for fifteen days, and then set out on his journey to Rome.

B: This is a puzzling statement to be found in *Le Verrier* (?) manuscript, as there is ample documentary information to prove that Pope Benedict XIII had, in 1403, authorized Bethencourt and Gadifer de la Salle to choose a clergyman to be appointed Bishop of the conquered islands. And thus, in 1404, he established the see of Rubicón and nominated Fray Alonso de Sanlúcar de Barrameda, a supporter of Avignon, Bishop of the same. If Bishop Alberto de las Casas ever existed, he must have been appointed in 1404, but by the Roman Pope Innocent VII. But this and the account that follows in *Le Verrier* (?) lacks documentary corroboration.

18.—DEATH OF BETHENCOURT

Bethencourt, now an old man, settled in Grainville with his young wife, Madame Fayel. He frequently received news from Maciot about his dear islands; and he lived in the hope of returning to his kingdom one day.

In 1425, he became seriously ill. So he drafted his will and was administered the last sacraments. He was buried in Grainville la Teinturiere, in the village church in front of the high altar, in 1425.

XXV.—The Orotava Valley, Tenerife.

XXVI.—Partial View of the Realejo coast, Tenerife.

XXVII.—Arucas, Gran Canaria.

XXVIII.—Santa Cruz de la Palma seen from the «Risco de la Concepción».

CHAPTER VIII

Subsequent Protective Policy of the Kings of Castile in the Conquest of the Canary Islands

1.—Maciot de Bethencourt's Administration and Subsequent Cession of the Canary Islands

2.—Various Transactions and Cessions Involving the Canary Islands

3.—Occupation of Gomera and Attempts at Invading the Other Islands

4.—Diego de Herrera's Enterprise

5.—Political Organization of the Islands of Tenerife, Gran Canaria, and La Palma in Pre-Conquest Days

1.—Maciot de Bethencourt's Administration and the Subsequent Cession of the Canary Islands

Maciot, the conqueror's nephew, proved at first to be a wise, good and benevolent ruler. His religious zeal, the energy shown in punishing the misdemeanours of some Europeans in Hierro, the establishment of Lanzarote's capital, which he called *Teguise* to honour the name of old King Guardafía's daughter, who had borne him several sons —the ancestors of the Canarian Bethencourts—, these things are all to his credit. But the noble ruler was to become a tyrant later on. He thought it necessary to carry to lamentable extremities strict measures, to subdue the rebellious insticts the natives had begun to show. He despotically exacted the *quinto* tax and sent armed bands to the coasts of Tenerife and Gran Canaria, where they captured natives and sold them later as slaves in Spain.

About this time, Fray Mendo de Diezma arrived in Lanzarote, to occupy the apostolic see of San Marcial left vacant by Don Alberto de las Casas's death. Maciot refused to take the advice of this wise prelate, who then denouced his tyrannical regime to Queen Catherine, regent of Castile during the minority of John II.

The Queen gave secret orders to Don Enrique de Guzmán, Count of Niebla, who immediately sent four armed caravels to the Canaries, manned by Pedro Barba del Campo, Lord of Castro Fuerte. They carried strict instructions to curb Maciot's despotic rule. Maciot was then forced to sign an agreement which deprived him of any authority over the islands, both conquered and unconquered. He hid his shame in Madeira, but not before he had entered into treasonable negotiations with Don Enrique, Infante of Portugal, to whom he had ceded his rights over the island of Lanzarote.

Maciot's disgraceful behaviour, parting with something which was not really his, was to entail a long series of struggles between the crowns of Portugal and Castile. John I of Portugal took the matter to Rome and Pope Eugene IV, supreme arbitrator in the affair, acknowledged the rights of John II of Castile after careful consideration.

2.—VARIOUS TRANSACTIONS AND CESSIONS INVOLVING THE CANARY ISLANDS

The Canary Islands were to change hands frequently during the twenty remaining years of Maciot's life, and even after his death in 1452. Their various owners, almost as soon as they had obtained these domains, tried to transfer them. Maciot had ceded his non-existant rights to Pedro Barba, to the Portuguese Infante, and to the Count of Niebla. Pedro Barba promptly transferred his rights to Fernan Pérez, who gave them back to Don Enrique de Guzman el Bueno, Count of Niebla. Niebla won fame for granting an exemption from servitude to the natives of the Canary Islands. He, in his turn, sold the islands to Guillen de las Casas.

Almost all these noblemen belonged to the Andalusian aristocracy, and they were not particularly inclined to exchange the dangerous glory of fighting the Moors for the less spectacular feats they could accomplish in the Atlantic islands. Thus, most of these rulers of the Canaries contented themselves with making a tour of the conquered islands and attempting a fruitles reconnaissance of the rest.

Henry IV of Castile later offered these islands to a Portuguese nobleman, the Count of Atouguia, who afterwards transferred his rights to one of his kinsmen, the Count of Villarreal. This latter ceded the Canaries to the Infante Don Fernando, Alfonso V of Portugal's brother.

Those constant cessions of a right which in truth belonged only to the first conqueror of the islands, who had left it in his will to his brother, Reinaldo de Bethencourt, gave rise to various controversies, duly recorded in the old chronicles.

Guillén de las Casas died in 1440 and, on his death, the Canaries came under the rule of Juan de las Casas's son-in-law Fernán Peraza, Lord of Valdeflores, who obtained these domains through his wife, Doña Inés de las Casas, daughter of the aforesaid Juan de las Casas. The new lord of the Canaries set off on a journey to the islands, accompanied by his son Guillén, a young man who had already given many proofs of his extraordinary bravery.

3.—OCCUPATION OF GOMERA AND ATTEMPTS AT INVADING THE OTHER ISLANDS

Fernán Peraza arrived at Lanzarote, where he had to fight the Portuguese who had attempted to settle in the island with the help of Prince Henry. Peraza withstood the Portuguese attacks and was forced to move his headquarters to Fuerteventura, Hierro, and Gomera, which he had already conquered.

Peraza could not settle in Gomera until after 1445. And even then the natives were still enjoying their independence, for this island, as we have said before, was not conquered but only subdued sometime after 1488. The truth was that Fernán Peraza, entrenched with his men in the famous tower of Gomera which he had built near San Sebastián, was hard pressed to resist the attacks of the rebellious natives.

The most significant event during Peraza's government was the expedition sent to the island of La Palma. Peraza furnished three men-of-war, which carried 200 Spanish crossbowmen and 300 natives armed with their typical weapons. Peraza's son was appointed leader of this expedition. Once having arrived at La Palma, Guillén set off on his journey into the wild interior. The natives were in command of all the gorges, from which heights they harassed the Spaniards by flinging huge stones at them. One of these mortally struck the gallant Don Guillén.

Martel, second in command, managed to carry Guillen's body aboard one of the ships, but not before he had lost several of his men. He then took his dead leader to Gomera, where young Guillén was idolized. The mournful song, that sad lips repeated the day he was buried, is a good example of how bitterly we do complain whem deprived of what we love most:

>Llorad las damas,
>si Dios os vala.
>Guillen Peraza
>quedó en La Palma,
>la flor marchita
>de la su cara.
>No eres Palma,
>eres retama,
>eres ciprés
>de triste rama;
>eres desdicha,
>desdicha mala.
>Tus campos rompan
>tristes volcanes,
>No vean placeres,
>sino pesares,
>cubran tus flores
>los arenales.
>¡Guillen Peraza!
>¡Guillen Peraza!
>¿Do está tu escudo?
>¿Do está tu lanza?
>Todo lo acaba
>la mala andanza.

Mourn, ladies, mourn, / God help you. / Guillen Peraza / was lost in La Palma, / the withered flower / of his face. / You are no Palm, / but broom / you are a cypress / with sad branches; / you are a misfortune, / a terrible misfortune. / May your fields be rent / by sad volcanoes, / may they witness no pleasure / but pain / may your flowers / be covered in sand. / Guillen Peraza! / Guillen Peraza! / Where is your shield? / Where is your spear? / Ill fate brings / everything to its sad end.

His comrades-in-arms could not surmount such a misfortune nor could his father, Fernan Peraza, who died shortly afterwards, in 1452, at Gomera.

4.—Diego de Herrera's Enterprise

The death of Guillen left Ines Peraza de las Casas, Fernan Peraza's daughter, direct heir to his domains. This lady had married the celebrated Diego García de Herrera, son of María de Ayala and Pedro García de Herrera, Marshall of Castile and Lord of Ampudia.

Doña Inés Peraza de las Casas and Diego de Herrera came into the vast domains of the Canary Islands. Both of them intended to pursue further the conquest and set in order the administration of their new lands, where the constant changing of rulers had fostered abuse and rebellion. They sailed for the Canaries in 1454 and took with them a fair company of noblemen, eager to help them in their enterprise, and seven Franciscan friars who established a convent in Fuerteventura. St. Diego de Alcalá became the custodian here.

Diego de Herrera had to uphold his rights in the teeth of Portuguese invasion, induced by Maciot's treason, until the Parliaments of Castile and Lisbon came to an agreement, acknowledging the rights of Doña Inés Peraza and her husband, Diego de Herrera. The affair was finally settled with the marriage of Don Diego de Silva, leader of the Portuguese expedition, to Doña María, Inés de Peraza's daughter. Once the legitimate rulers of the island were freed from such a dangerous competitor, they directed all their efforts to the arduous task of conquering the rest of the archipelago.

Herrera sent an expedition against Gran Canaria in 1461. But these intrepid men, placed under the command of Herrera's son-in-law, Diego de Silva, would have perished, crushed by the superiority in number of their enemies, had not the *Guanarteme* of Galdar generously protected them from the violence of his people. The *Guanarteme* surrendered himself to the Spaniards, pretending that these would kill him if they were not allowed to retreat. Seeing his attempts at invasion thwarted, Herrera started negotiations with this king in the

Telde district. He was allowed to build a fortress there. But the natives soon realized that the newcomers were intent on becoming the lords of the island, and finally attacked the garrison and killed the Spaniards. To achieve this end, they had recourse to a wily trick: they dressed themselve as Spaniards, using the clothes of those they had captured, so that when those in the fortress rushed to meet them, in the belief that they were welcoming their saviours, they met an instant death at the hands of the treacherous natives.

The attempt to conquer Tenerife in 1464, led also by Herrera, bore similar results. He did not dare to start hostilities in view of the reduced number of his troops. So, he decided to befriend the natives instead. His peace offerings were accepted, and the natives did not mind the complicated ceremonies by which he pretended to annex the island to the crown of Castile. Nor did they object to the building of a fortress there. But the very recklessness of the Europeans soon brought such a happy harmony to an end; and the newcomers had to leave Tenerife in haste.

This barren war, which Herrera's warlike enthusiasm forced upon them, could not but awaken the discontent of the Canarian people. They rebelled against his despotic power and made their complaints heard at Court, so that the Catholic Monarchs summoned Diego de Herrera and his wife to the peninsula. The old rights of Juan de Bethencourt were once again unearthed, and it turned out that these rights should have returned to the Crown of Castile, as no legitimate heir to the conqueror had claimed them after his death.

The people of Lanzarote mutinied. They took justice into their own hands and Teguise witnessed many bloody encounters. Juan Mayor and Juan de Armas bitterly complained to the Catholic King and Queen, who immediately commanded an account of the events from Esteban Pérez de Cabitos. In 1477, in their attempt to end discontent and insurrection, Ferdinand and Isabella assumed the conquest of the remaining islands: Gran Canaria, Tenerife, and La Palma.

The report was submitted to Fray Hernando de Talavera, and the lawyers Juan and Rodrigo, who were of the opinion that Herrera and his wife had full rights to the domain, possession, and sovereignty over the islands of Lanzarote, Fuerteventura, Hierro, and Gomera, though subjected to the supreme rights the Crown exercised over all the lands, villages, and domains belonging to the realm's noblemen. Herrera and his wife had likewise lawful rights to the conquest of Gran Canaria, Tenerife, and La Palma —granted by special privilege to Alfonso de las Casas, Doña Ines's ancestor, by King John II. Thus, if a just and reasonable cause prompted the monarchs to undertake the conquest of the aforesaid islands, Diego de Herrera and his wife would have to be compensated for the expense and effort which they had incurred in accomplishing it.

On October 15th, 1477, a contract of cession was drawn up at Seville, before Bartolomé Sánchez de Porras and by it, Herrera and Inés relinquished their rights over the islands of Gran Canaria, Tenerife, and La Palma. It was also agreed that the Royal Exchequer would finance the conquest, and would pay Herrera an indemnity of 5,000,000 maravedises for renouncing his rights and for all the expenses he had incurred. Herrera was also granted the title of Count of Gomera to compensate him for the loss of his dreams of conquest.

Though prevented from showing his warlike talents in the Atlantic islands, Diego de Herrera was to become famous for his prowess in the Barbary coasts, where his very name terrified the African princes.

It is not hyperbolic to say that the fate of the unconquered islands was sealed when Ferdinand and Isabella resolved to undertake their conquest. But the three islands not yet annexed to the Spanish Crown were the most difficult to subdue. Though some sections of the population would not prove hostile to the conquerors, the struggle about to begin, the hardest and longest until then, was an enterprise worthy of the illustrious Catholic Monarchs.

This marked the second stage in the conquest of the Canaries. However, before entering into the events that culminated in the annexation of the islands to the Spanish Crown, it would be enlightening to delve into a brief survey of the political organization of these islands, so that the immense effort that the subjugation of this indomitable people entailed is better understood.

5.—POLITICAL ORGANIZATION OF THE ISLANDS OF TENERIFE, GRAN CANARIA, AND LA PALMA IN PRE-CONQUEST DAYS

According to the few traditional accounts that have survived, the island of Tenerife was at one time ruled by one king. The last of the Menceyes, *Tinerfe el Grande* had his court at Adeje. His firstborn, *Bentinerfe* or *Bentenuhya*, unwilling to wait until his father's death to ascend the throne, rebelled against him. His eight brothers followed suit. Then, they divided among themselves the old Adeje monarchy and brought about the death of the unhappy *Tinerfe*. The nine new kingdoms were given the names of: *Tahoro, Gúimar, Abona, Adeje, Daute, Icod, Tacoronte, Tegueste,* and *Naga* or *Anaga*.

Bentenuhya, more ambitious and dauntless than his brothers, obtained the *Tahoro* district and with it the position of first *Mencey* of the island. *Imobach* came after him and attempted to re-establish the absolute monarchy of his grandfather's time. His kinsmen, however, opposed his designs. *Bencomo, Imobach's* son, succeeded him and his gallantry and courage were to win him a special place in the annals of the conquest.

Tinerfe's other sons and their descendents ruled in the following chronological order:

Acaymo, mencey of Gúimar, proved a firm ally of the Europeans and his son, *Añaterve*, pursued his father's policy —helping the conquerors in countless moments of peril.

Atguaxoña, mencey of Abona, was an obscure ruler who was succeeded by his son, *Atxoña*, an inept and stupid prince who resented Bencomo's power to the point of refusing to join the league against the Spaniards, thus contributing to the final loss of the island.

Atbitocazpe ruled over the old domain of Adeje. The seat of this *menceyato* stood where the capital of the island is now. *Pelinor, Atbitocazpe's* son, succeeded him and, led by his blind trust, he followed the misguided advice of the mencey of Abona, and was unable to withstand the attacks of the conquerors by himself.

Caconaymo King of the Daute states in the eastern part of the island and *Rosmen,* his heir, were first opposed to the league, thinking themselves free from danger. But *Rosmen* cowardly sued for peace once he realized his folly.

Pelinor, son and successor of *Chincanayro,* mencey of Icod, was likewise envious of Bencomo's power and refused to enter the alliance.

Rumen, mencey of the fertile district of Tacoronte, was succeeded by his son, *Acaymo,* one of the ablest champions in the fight for independence.

Tegueste I obtained the district to which he later gave his name. He was famous for his many herds of cattle, which, it was rumored, needed 100 shepherds. His son, *Tegueste II,* proved a formidable leader in the war against Spain.

Serdeto or *Beneharo I* was the youngest son of *Tinerfe* and mencey of Anaga. The Spaniards attacked this mencey first, soon realizing how dangerous he could be. His son, *Beneharo II,* was both a staunch ally of *Bencomo* and one of the most fearless defenders of his country.

We must also make mention of *Aguahuco,* the bastard son of *Tinerfe,* who was given the title of *Achimencey* (impoverished nobleman) because of the smallness of his state. It was situated in the northern part of the island and still preserves its old name: *Punta del Hidalgo. Aguahuco's* son and heir, *Sebenzuí* or *Zebenzayas,* was to become an almost mythical figure for his courage in the island's traditions.

When the Spanish troops arrived, led by the Adelantado Don Alonso Fernández de Lugo, the island was thus divided: *Añatarve,* mencey of Gúimar; *Atxoña,* mencey of Abona; *Pelinor,* mencey of Adeje; *Rosmen,* mencey of Daute; *Pelicar,* mencey of Tegueste; *Beneharo II,* mencey of Anaga; and *Sebenzuí,* lord of Punta del Hidalgo. All of them were independent rulers and commanded a good number of warriors, but the mencey of Tahoro, *Quehebi Bencomo Inobach,* whose domains were the richest and most populated, and whose forces were the most numerous —9,000 men according to a reliable estimate— was considered the sovereign of them all.

The island of Gran Canaria had suffered a political evolution along opposite lines. Some years before the European invasion, it had been divided into ten independent tribes, each under a different chieftain: *Galdar, Telde, Agüimes, Tejeda, Aquejata, Agaete, Tamaraceite, Artebirgo, Artiacar,* and *Arucas.*

But a remarkable queen, noted for her wisdom and superb beauty, united the different principalities. This bold and intelligent heroine was called *Andamana.* She proclaimed herself elightened by divine inspiration, and people blindly believed in her predictions and had a boundles faith in her advice. *Andamana* could not but have her detractors —as all great men and women throughout history— who envied her power and tried to discredit her in the eyes of her people. She discovered a plot to overthrow her and sought to secure a powerful ally by marrying *Gumidafe,* one of the bravest warriors of Galdar. *Gumidafe,* at the head of a small army, managed to subdue all the tribes in the island. Thus the old oligarchy was replaced by a centralized monarchy.

Gumidafe and *Andamana* were proclaimed *Guanartemes* of Gran Canaria and they established their court at Galdar. According to historical accounts, they died towards the end of the fourteenth century.

Artemi Semidan, their successor, possessed his father's courage and soon gave proof of it by defeating the first European invaders. Adventurers and pirates came first to the island during his reign, and the prince quickly showed them the bravery of which the Canarians are capable. According to tradition, he died in the battle of Arguineguín in 1405, during Bethencourt's luckless expedition.

Artemi's sons, *Tenesor Semidan* and *Bentaguayre Semidan,* were proclaimed Guanartemes, and divided the island into two kingdoms. *Tenesor* ruled over Galdar, from Tamaraceite to the valley which is now called *Aldea de San Nicolás*. This included the districts of Arguineguín and Tunte. *Bentaguayre's* dominions were Telde and the cantons of Argones, Cendro, and Agúimes. Both states, though independent, remained united for some time because of economic reasons.

Although Bentaguayre's domains were the richest, he resolved to usurp his brother's throne. This unbridled ambition led him to recruit 10,000 men and invade the Galdar principality. With 4,000 men hastily summoned to help him, *Tenesor* outwitted and defeated his brother.

Tenesor's power was once more in peril when *Doramas, guayre* or minister of his council, an able man who had achieved considerable popularity, rebelled against him. The rebels had few hopes of success when the death of *Bentaguayre* gave a sudden turn to the outcome of the rebellion. *Doramas* then abandoned his original plan and seized Telde instead. There he ruled until the conquest.

The island of La Palma was the smallest of the three islands yet unconquered and, according to Father Abreu Galindo, it was then called *Benahoare* (my country) by the natives. It was divided into twelve kingdoms: to the west were *Aridane, Tihuya,* and *Tamanaca;* to the east were *Abenguareme, Tigalate, Tedote, Tenagua,* and *Adeyahamen;* to the north were *Tagaragre, Galguen,* and *Tiscaguan;* and in the midlands was *Eceró* or *Aceró*. Each of the districts was ruled by its own prince.

Mutual rivalry had given rise to frequent bloody encounters in these cantons. In such a divided country, dissension and conflict must have been rampant. Tradition has preserved a confused memory of the terrible wars between *Echentive,* prince of Abenguareme, and *Mayatingo,* king of Aridane, who lost one of his arms in them and was then nicknamed *Aganeye,* «the one with the arm cut off».

Notwithstanding their warlike spirit, these islanders have been accused of cowardice by Núñez de la Peña and Espinosa.

But other historians, such as Viera y Clavijo and Abreu Galindo, fully acknowledge the bravery of the Palmeños.

In truth, the natives of La Palma successfully withstood every attempt at invasion until the late fifteenth century; and if most of the tribes showed but a weak opposition to Don Alonso Fernández de Lugo, this was due to the advantageous terms offered by the Spanish nobleman, and their naive belief in the force of these treatises.

United in a common front against the invader, they proved invincible for quite a long time. Bethencourt and his men could not secure an inch of the island, and later on Guillén Peraza, who tried to conquer it with a considerable army, was defeated at the first attempt, losing his life in the bargain.

Viera y Clavijo accurately called the people La Palma the Spartans of the Canaries. Their courage in the battlefield and their patriotic love, of which they gave so many proofs, clearly remind us of the Greek heroes in classical times.

This brief account of the political organization in the three islands, and the bravery of the natives, will suffice to illustrate the many difficulties the conquerors found in their path, and how arduous was the task of subduing the three most warlike islands in the archipelago.

The Catholic Monarchs Undertake the Conquest of the Islands of Gran Canaria, Tenerife, and La Palma

A. - The Conquest of Gran Canaria.

1.—Juan Rejón's Expedition
2.—Battle of Guiniguada
3.—Dissensions between Rejón and Dean Bermúdez
4.—The attack on Tirajana
5.—Juan Rejón Returns to the Canaries
6.—Juan Rejón Is Discharged and Repaced by Pedro de Vera
7.—Pedro de Vera's First Political Moves
8.—Death of Doramas
9.—The Agaete Fortress is Built. Second Battle of Tirajana
10.—Return and Death of Juan Rejón
11.—The Attack on Galdar. Subjection of its Guanarteme
12.—Further Exploits Performed by Pedro de Vera
13.—Gran Canaria Is Conquered At Last
14.—Uprisings in Gomera and Death of Hernán Peraza, Son of Diego de Herrera

XXIX.—Parish church of El Salvador, and architectural masterpiece from the sixteenth century, Santa Cruz de la Palma.

XXX.—Los Tilos, at San Andrés y Sauces, Island of La Palma.

XXXI.—The caves of Las Cruces and the hermitage of Valerón, historical remains of the Guanche «habitat», Las Palmas.

XXXII.—The Tejada Valley and the Roque Nublo in Gran Canaria.

1.—Juan Rejón's Expedition

As we said at the beginning of Chapter VII, when the Catholic King and Queen undertook the conquest of the Canaries, the second stage in the conquest of the Archipelago started.

Gran Canaria, often celebrated for its luxuriant woods, its shadowy grottos, embellished by tall and impressive trees, was first sighted by Juan Rejón on 24 June, 1478. Ferdinand and Isabella had entrusted this brave soldier with the difficult task of conquering the island. Rejón, who had been appointed Captain-General of the Conquest, recruited 600 infantrymen and secured 30 horses in Seville, Cadiz, and neighbouring villages.

Several noblemen enlisted as volunteers in the expedition and were regarded as second in command. Among them we may mention the *Alférez Mayor* Alonso Jáimez de Sotomayor, who was appointed standard-bearer, and Juan Bermúdez, Dean of Rubicón. On 28 May, 1478, they left Puerto de Santa María and on 24 June of the same year they disembarked at the beach of Isleta.

Only the outstanding events in the conquest will be touched upon, without entering into the sordid details of the various dissensions and envies which so often remind the reader of the American enterprise.

Viera refers how the first thing this conquering army did was to attend mass, using a hut made of palm trees as chapel. Then, full of hope and trusting in God's mercy, they marched towards the fortress built by Herrera. At this point, an old Canarian woman appeared and encouraged the Spanish general to set up camp at the entrance to the ravine of Guiniguada.

The soldiers quickly deemed her intervention miraculous, as the place to which they were thus directed could not have been more pleasant, richer in water, palm and fig trees. Las Palmas, that beautiful city the Canarians are justly proud of, was to stand, in years to come, on that very place.

2.—The Battle of Guiniguada

The arrival of the Spanish troops at Telde set the district in a state of alarm. Energetic Doramas was the ruler there at the time and he quickly sent notice to the most important noblemen, prepared for the defence of the district, and encouraged his people. He reminded them of the glorious death of bold Artemi and, assembling a force of more than 2,000 men, helped by the courageous Adargoma, *Guayre* of Galdar, he marched towards the Guiniguada river and attacked the Spanish camp.

Juan Rejón, eager to win a respite in order to finish building his fortifications, sent an envoy to Doramas with protestations of friendship, but this haughty prince merely answered: «Tell your captain that tomorrow I will bring him my reply.»

Thus, next day's dawn was for war, not peace. This early attack placed the Spaniards at a disadvantage, as they were not yet ready to fight from their trenches. But Rejón, realizing that the negotiations with which he hoped to win time would prove fruitless, was forced to fight. He divided his scanty troops into three sections: the left wing was placed under the command of Captain Rodrigo de Solórzano, the right wing under Captain Alonso Fernández de Lugo, and the centre forces were commanded by Rejón himself. The cavalry was entrusted to Dean Bermúdez, with Alonso Jáimez de Sotomayor as bearer of the Royal Standard.

Their enemies did not offer such an ordered formation. However, they vastly outnumbered the Spaniards and they also had 500 warriors armed with spears and bucklers, obtained no doubt from previous attempts at invasion. The bravery of leaders like Maninidra, *Guayre* of Tazarta and Adargoma, prince of Galdar, was an added asset.

After four hours of fighting, no substantial advantages had been won by either party. The natives attacked the left wing but Rejón quickly came to their aid, wounded Adargoma with a thrust of his spear, and took him prisoner. The loss of their leader increased the fury of the Canarians, but Doramas, seeing the bravest of his men fall and aware of the more advantageous position of the Spaniards in the trenches, and the carnage made by their cannons and horses, resolved to retreat, leaving 300 dead on the battlefield and with a larger number of wounded among his men. On the Spanish side, the losses were not severe —only seven were dead and twenty five wounded.

Thus ended the famous battle of Guiniguada, one of the most celebrated in the annals of the conquest of Gran Canaria. With it, the fate of the island was sealed.

3.—Dissensions Between Rejón and Dean Bermúdez

The high hopes inspired by the Guiniguada victory were somehow dampened by the growing enmity between Rejón and Canon Juan Bermúdez, Dean of San Marcial de Rubicón in Lanzarote. Bermúdez, Rejón's main antagonist, took advantage of the situation to rally a powerful party opposed to the general. The conquest had reached a point of stagnation. Victuals were very expensive, and they blamed Rejón for all the misfortunes they were experiencing, for they maintained that things were deteriorating due to his incompetent administration. Rejón, in an attempt to pacify them, set sail for Lanzarote, where he hoped to obtain Herrera's help. Herrera however did not accept Rejón's reasons for the voyage and refused to come to his aid.

Meanwhile, Bermúdez availed himself of Rejón's absence and wrote to Spain requesting the appointment of a military governor and an investigation of Rejón's behaviour. The Spanish Crown sent Pedro de Algaba, who sided with Bermúdez and had Rejón carried to the peninsula in chains and fetters. But the unfortunate leader managed to clear his name at Court and returned to the Canary Islands to avenge such an outrage.

Three ships furnished with victuals, ammunition and some new recruits, were placed under his command. He was also accompanied in this expedition by the new bishop of Rubicón, Juan Frías. But on arriving at the *Real de las Palmas*, not even the conciliatory moves of this bishop could bring Rejón's enemies to terms. Governor Algaba and Canon Bermúdez prevented the general from coming ashore, and Rejón was forced to return to the *Cadiz*, one of the vessels of his small fleet.

4.—THE ATTACK ON TIRAJANA

Governor Algaba, unwilling to see his troops inactive and availing himself of the fresh forces which had just arrived from Spain, set off on a new expedition with Bishop Frías in 1479.

The Spaniards cast anchor off the coast of Arguineguín, disembarked, and proceeded unmolested as far as the valley of Tirajana. But when on their way back to the ships, they were ambushed at the gorges neat the coast. Twenty died, one hundred were wounded, and eighty were taken prisoners. The captives, however, were soon released, thanks to the generosity of the Guanarteme of Telde. The battle of Tirajana was in part to compensate the natives for the Guiniguada defeat.

5.—JUAN REJÓN RETURNS TO THE CANARIES

Meanwhile, the Catholic Monarchs had offered proper satisfaction to Juan Rejón for the injuries that he had endured. The Spanish Court endowed Rejón with unlimited powers to maintain his authority and punish his enemies, if necessary. A ship was placed at his disposal and the conqueror returned to the islands for the third time. On 2 May, 1480, he arrived at Isleta, and that very night he went ashore with the thirty soldiers he had brought from Spain. He sent a secret communication to his brother-in-law, Alonso Jáimez de Sotomayor, and to the governor of the garrison, a close friend of his, Pérez de Cabitos. The three quickly reached an agreement, and at dawn, Rejón and his men stormed into the *Real de las*

Palmas. They entered the Cathedral crying: «God save the King!»

Taken by surprise, Algaba rose at once and made for the Cathedral in an attempt to re-establish order, but he was soon arrested and taken to the tower. Canon Bermúdez and some of his supporters suffered the same fate. The orders given to the Captain-General by the Catholic Kings were read out aloud at the parade grounds. The flourish of trumpets and bugles accompanied the announcement of the supreme authority of Juan Rejón. Algaba was tried by court martial and beheaded at the Main Square, while people watched in terror and awe. Bermúdez was banished first to Lanzarote and then to Malaga's Cathedral.

6.—Juan Rejón is Discharged and Replaced by Pedro de Vera

Algaba's execution was to cause Rejón to be discharged. Queen Isabella, moved by the sorrow of the unhappy widow and her sons, thought that the punishment had been unjust and appointed Pedro de Vera in Rejón's place. Pedro de Vera was an Andalusian nobleman, lord lieutenant of Jerez de la Frontera and governor of the garrison of Jimena. He had been brought up at the court of Henry III of Castile, and was now appointed governor of Gran Canaria and Captain-General of the Conquest. Vera left Cadiz with three other ships, one hundred and fifty crossbowmen, and fifty horses. He arrived at Las Palmas on 18 August, 1480, and took command of the city. Rejón was recalled to the peninsula.

7.—Pedro de Vera's First Political Moves

Treason was to mark the first steps of Vera in the Canaries. This all the more intensified the growing hatred of the natives towards the Spaniards. When Vera arrived in Las Palmas, more than 200 natives, who had been converted, used to come to the Spanish camp as friends. But Vera, distrustful of such amiable overtures and afraid of running short of victuals, persuaded the islanders to go on board one of his ships which, he told them, would sail for Tenerife to undertake the conquest of the islands. But the general had secretly ordered the captain of the ship to take the islanders to Spain, where they were to be sold as slaves. It was not until they were at sea that the truth dawned upon the unfortunate captives. They hijacked the crew to Lanzarote. There, Herrera welcomed them warmly.

8.—The Death of Doramas

The death of Doramas cannot go unmentioned. We must not forget that he was the first distinguished leader to appear in the annals of the conquest of the Canaries.

Pedro de Vera decided to break hostilities and stationed his troops in the mountains of Arucas. Doramas, leader of the Telde forces, took positions with his men in the nearby heights and, trusting in his own courage, sent the Spanish general a summons to fight: «If among those effeminate foreigners there is one who dares to fight with me, the battle may be spared.» Vera promptly accepted the challenge, but his men dissuaded him from entering the battlefield alone.

Juan de Hozes charged on his Andalusian horse and severly wounded the Canarian prince from behind. The wounded Doramas broke the Spaniard's leg with a side blow, but Vera took advantage of this and thrusted a spear through Doramas' breast. The bold prince fell on his knees but had enough strenght left to utter, «You would never have defeated me if that traitor had not attacked me from behind.» Then, twice wounded and bleeding profusely, he started shouting for water. Viera y Clavijo said that water was brought in an iron helmet and Doramas was baptized there and then. But Marin y Cubas maintained that the prince was merely thirsty, and not because he was eager to enter the way of salvation. Doramas died almost on drinking that water.

The annals record: «The whole army attended the funeral rites. His body was handed over to the Canarians who buried him in the famous mountain which bears his name up to this date. Thus, he, who had reached pre-eminence through his courage and resplendent virtues, died at the height of his glory. His mournful country was to call him the *last of the Canarians*.»

9.—THE AGAETE FORTRESS IS BUILT. THE SECOND BATTLE OF TIRAJANA

Aware of the strategic importance of an outpost near the western coast, Vera had the Agaete fortress built in 1481, where he left a garrison consisting of fifty infantrymen and ten horses, under the command of Alonso Fernández de Lugo. Soon after this, he sent a battalion to Tirajana, dislodging the natives of this district, who had sought the impregnable refuge of the crags.

The Spaniards launched an attack but the stones hurled by their foes forced them to retreat, leaving twenty five men on the field. This setback prompted the Captain-General to send reinforcements and, in spite of so many difficulties, the Spaniards managed to capture the enemy positions.

Notwithstanding this Spanish victory, the courage and patriotism of the natives remained unabated. Bentaguayre continuously harassed the Real de las Palmas: «His strategems match his temerity. He takes the sentries by surprise, gets into the Spanish camp at night, butchers Vera's horses and sets everything in a state of alarm with his unexpected attacks.»

10.—RETURN AND DEATH OF JUAN REJÓN

While Vera was busy with these events, Rejón had obtained the royal pardon and an appointment as Adelantado, in charge of the conquest of Tenerife and La Palma. But this enterprise was aborted due to the assasination of the Spanish leader in Gomera.

Hernán Peraza, son of Don Diego de Herrera and governor of Gomera, appeared at first to have been behind the henious crime. Doña Elvira de Sotomayor, Rejón's widow, left at once for Seville where she begged the monarchs to punish her husband's assassin. Hernán Peraza was summoned back to court, where he was asked to give an account of what happened. Through the help of his numerous and influential kinsmen, he was acquitted from the charges brought against him.

Queen Isabella gave him the lovely Beatriz de Bobadilla to marry —the girl being the niece of her own lady-in-waiting— and his sole penalty amounted to the duty of providing Diego de Vera with a company of soldiers to help him in the conquest of Gran Canaria.

11.—The Attack on Galdar. Subjection of its Guanarteme

Hernán Peraza, on his return voyage to the Canaries, visited the Agaete fortress, which had recently been built at Galdar in Gran Canaria. Alonso Fernández de Lugo, marshall of the garrison, was eager to put to good use such welcome reinforcements. He joined forces with Hernán Peraza and, under cover of night, launched an attack on that district. Their enemies, taken by surprise on the Artinara road, were promptly defeated. He captured the Guanarteme Tenesor Semidán, the renowned Maninidra, and other Guayres, seizing also a rich booty.

The conquerors were to profit highly from such a feat. Tenesor and his guayres were sent to Spain to be presented as war trophies to the Catholic Kings. The unfortunate guanarteme and his men arrived at the Spanish court, where they were lavishly entertained. Tenesor then asked to be baptized, and Cardinal Pedro González de Mendoza performed the rites at Toledo Cathedral, with the Catholic King acting as godfather.

The Guanarteme and his gauyres, accompanied by Ferdinand and Isabella, visited then the Spanish towns. Wherever he went, the royal captive was treated with the utmost respect. He dressed in garments of purple silk, which the king had given him, and the Spanish sovereign tactfully provided the guayres with robes according to their rank.

Tenesor Semidán, whom the historians of the conquest called *Don Fernando Guanarteme* after his baptism, was sent back to Gran Canaria in October, 1482. He was then asked to persuade his subjects to submit to Spanish rule.

12.—Further Exploits Performed by Pedro de Vera

Don Fernando Guanarteme proved a valuable ally. Vera took advantage of the situation and this, together with the fresh troops which had just been sent from Spain, incited him to attack the fortified positions which the fearless islanders defended in 1482. Their leader was Bentejuí, who had been proclaimed guanarteme, and he, supported by the guayres Tazarte and Hercher Hamenat, was ready to continue the war.

Don Fernando tried in vain to dissuade his fellow-countrymen from waging war against his new friends. He vividly depicted the power and magnificent of the Catholic Monarchs, but the answer he got from the Canarians may be exemplified by the message they sent him: «You, whom we had surnamed the Good, have betrayed us to our enemies. Alas, corrupted guanarteme, unworthy of your race and your name, go back to those scoundrels who have duped you. Go back to them and flatter those hungry dogs!» Don Fernando argued that he had been but a prisoner of war and that they, had they been in his position, would have behaved in the same way. But bold Tazarte answered him thus: «Stay with us, win back your dignity; here you will find men ready to fight and die. Canaria is not yet annihilated. Look, she will always stand, forever on these mountains.»

Those courageous islanders were to put up a desperate resistance. The victory of Bentayga was a measure of their bravery. Vera, who had to retreat on that occasion, won the day at Titana, in the vicinity of Cendro. He took the mountains of Adójar, and on that eve the Canarian women were seen hurling themselves from the top of those crags, to escape captivity. Tazarte, realizing that everything was lost once Aytami had surrendered, threw himself into the sea from the Tirma heights.

13.—Gran Canaria is Conquered at Last

Eager to bring the Canarians into total subjection, Pedro de Vera attacked Adojár, where the remaining defenders had sought refuge. Miguel de Mujica and most of his Biscayans lost their lives in the encounter. These combats were but the last and resplendent achievements of Canarian heroism.

Don Fernando Guanarteme was sent as a peace envoy to the rebels who kept the Ansite valley. The islanders were persuaded by their old Guanarteme to cast off their weapons, and begged Don Fernando to take them before the Spanish general. But Bentejuí and the *Faycan*, or high priest, refusing to endure such an ignominy, climbed the Ansite mountain and, in a final tribute to heroism and patriotism and crying *Atis tirma!*, jumped into the sea.

Guayarmina, Bentejuí's bride and Fernando de Guanarteme's daughter, had in the meantime arrived at the Spanish camp. Accompanied by two unarmed Canarians, she was brought before the Spanish general to whom she said: «We poor islanders, an independent people until this date, are ready to submit to the Catholic Kings, and place ourselves and our possessions under the protection of our new sovereign.»

Thus was the conquest of Gran Canaria accomplished on 29 April, 1483. Bishop Frías sang a *Te Deum* and Lieutenant Alonso Jáimez de Sotomayor, hoisting the royal standard, uttered the victory cries from the top of the camp's tower.

Once the island was pacified, the conquerors received their equitable share of lands. Don Fernando Guanarteme and other islanders were graciously granted some estates by the Spanish monarchs.

Spanish rule brought about a complete change. Where the *Real de las Palmas* had stood, a town was built. Graced with the dignity of «villa», it became and still is the capital of the island. The tiny Rubicón Cathedral was moved to the new city, Las Palmas. Arts and crafts imported from the Continent opened new roads to progress and culture. Agriculture was promoted and new vegetal species, hitherto unknown to the Canaries, were acclimatized. Meanwhile, trade had contributed to civilization. The increase in the island's wealth was due, in part, to this economic boom.

14.—Uprisings in Gomera and Death of Hernán Peraza, Son of Diego de Herrera

Pedro de Vera was quietly enjoying his victory when, towards 1488, peace in Gomera was unsettled by serious disturbances, which culminated in the assassination of Hernán Peraza.

Hernán Peraza had been for some time carrying on a secret affair with beautiful Yballa, a young Canarian from the Guahedun canton. When the clandestine affair reached the ears of Hautacuperche, Yballa's suitor, he conspired with some Mulagua tribesmen and resolved to seize the lord of the island and force him into a formal avowal to deal more fairly with the natives. Once set upon this, the occasion soon arose on which they would be able to fulfill their plans.

Peraza sent word to Yballa, through the girl's old nurse, that she was to meet him at the Guahedun cave. The Gomerytes, under the leadership of Hautacuperche, waited in the vicinity of the cave for Peraza. But Yballa sensed the danger and warned him. Peraza quickly donned his cuirass, grabbed his weapons, and went out to meet the rebels. Hautacuperche, who stood on top of the cave, killed the Spaniard with his javelin. Two page boys were also slain, and this massacre was to mark the opening of the rebellion.

Doña Beatriz de Bobadilla, Peraza's widow, was compelled to seek the shelter of the tower where she remained with her family and some faithful natives. Led once again by Hautacuperche, the rebels lay siege to the tower, but Doña Beatriz's men courageously withstood the attacks and managed to kill the leader with their crossbows.

Meanwhile, Pedro de Vera, informed by Doña Beatriz of what had happened, arrived at Gran Canaria with 400 veteran soldiers. The cruelty of his reprisals knew no bounds, and it appears that such atrocities were due to Doña Beatriz's vindictiveness. Gómez Escudero wrote:

«Once the rebels were captured and they admitted to having killed Hernan Peraza, though few had taken part in the actual deed, many were condemned to death. And all those above fifteen years of age were executed. They died of many different deaths, for some were hanged, others impaled, or dragged by horses. Some were cast into the sea with weights around their necks, and others had their feet and hands lopped off alive. It was a great pity to see Pedro de Vera indulging in such cruelty. He gave children as slaves to whomever he pleased; and he also sent a ship full of youngsters to be sold and the profits to be used in paying the soldiers. He summoned all the natives of Gomera who lived in Gran Canaria and who had arrived there accompanying their Lord in his Conquest. These too were regarded as accomplices in the rebellion. They were more than 300 in number, but he was careful not to spread such news and, once justice had been done, he left Gomera for Canaria where he ordered the conquerors in Guía, Telde, Arucas, and other places to arrest the Gomerytes. They were to suffer the same horrible fate as their fellow islanders. Many a scaffold and many an empalement had its full share of bodies. Plenty of them were carried in ships very far from the coast and then cast off into the sea bound hand and feet.»

Bishop Don Miguel López de la Cerna sent his horrified complaints to the Spanish Court and Diego de Vera was removed from his office and substituted by Francisco de Maldonado. Pedro de Vera acquired afterwards high renown in the siege of Granada and died in Spain when, having obtained the royal pardon and the restitution of his former dignity and domains, was about to return to the Canary Islands.

Pliny, the Latin encyclopedist, spoke about Gran Canaria as if it had just been recently discovered and added that it was given the name «Canaria» because of the great number of dogs found there.

CHAPTER X

B.- The Conquest of La Palma and Tenerife

1.—Alonso Fernández de Lugo is Appointed Captain-General of the Unconquered Islands
2.—First Tactical Moves in La Palma
3.—Attack on the Caldera and the Island's Surrender
4.—The Landing at Tenerife, Early Skirmishes
5.—The Guanche Princes League Together
6.—The Battle of Acentejo
7.—The Attack on the Tower of the Encampment. Retreat to Gran Canaria
8.—A Further Expedition Against the Guanches. Battle of La Laguna
9.—Further Progress of the Conquering Army. Plague Decimates the Guanches
10.—The Feat of the Twelve Soldiers
11.—Food Shortage at the Spanish Camp. Lópe Hernández de la Guerra's generous gesture
12.—The Second Battle of Acentejo
13.—The Spaniards Invade the Valley of Arautapola and Tenerife is Finally Conquered

1.—Alonso Fernández de Lugo is Appointed Captain-General of the Unconquered Islands

Upon Vera's departure, Alonso Fernández de Lugo, a native of Galicia but living in Seville, gradually came into the public light as the hero to whom the difficult enterprise of conquering La Palma and Tenerife was reserved. Lugo was one of the best soldiers of his time. His splendid military career had started in the Granadan wars. He was to gain further warlike experience in the conquest of Gran Canaria, where he had fought under Juan Rejón and Vera.

Ever since Gran Canaria had been pacified, Lugo had retained the estates he had obtained at the partition. But such a tranquil life could not satisfy for long a man trained from youth in the exercise of arms. Thus one day, he left his Canarian fortress for Spain, where he beseeched the Catholic Monarchs to confer upon him the honour of attempting the conquest of Tenerife and La Palma.

In 1492, at the Santa Fe encampment, where Columbus visited the Catholic Monarchs, Lugo obtained from Queen Isabella the license to embark on the conquest of the islands. He was provided with money and ships to be equipped at Cadiz. Upon arriving at Gran Canaria, the most important Spanish gentlemen living there and the leading islanders volunteered to take part in the expedition. Among them were: Maninidra, the old guayres Ibone, Ydutidana, and Fernando Guanarteme with fifty of his kinsmen.

Once the forces had been properly organized, two ships and a frigate took them to the rugged coasts of La Palma, where they arrived towards the end of September, 1492.

2.—First Tactical Moves in La Palma

Lugo had thought it advisable to attack this island first for, though he knew of the fierceness of its inhabitants and the difficulty of the terrain, he deemed it less populated and strong than Tenerife. He reached Aridane, one of the twelve cantons of La Palma, and landed on its beach.

The frequent contacts between the natives of La Palma and those from conquered Hierro greatly aided Lugo. It may even be said that this close relationship was an important step towards the final subjugation of the island. The Herrenians had already smoothed Lugo's path. Special mention must be made of one early ally, Francisca Gazmira, a Palmenian woman. Thus, it is not difficult to understand why Lugo's proposals to Prince Mayatinga were almost instantly accepted. These proposals, according to Viera y Clavijo, were summarized in four points: 1. There would be peace, concord, work, and friendship between the Spaniards and the Palmenians; 2. Mayatinga would pay homage to the Catholic Monarchs and would obey their commands as a vassal, though he would keed his princely rank and the rule of the Aridane district; 3. He and all his vassals would embrace Christianity; 4. He and his people would enjoy the same franchises and privileges as the Spanish vassals.

The chivalrous behaviour of Lugo while the negotiations were under way greatly helped in winning to his cause the main body of the Haonarytha tribes. Their leaders promptly accepted the same terms Lugo had offered the prince of Aridane. «These leaders were: Echedey, Tamanca, Echentive, and Azuquache, who ruled over the tribes or principalities of Tihuya, Guecheves, and Abenguareme.»

Lugo was quick to seal the friendship these leaders offered him. He asked for little compensation in return. His humane conduct was a powerful weapon, but no less powerful was his military prowess, for he had to fight Jariguo and Garehagua, the princes of Tigalate. There, the Spanish General was far from welcomed. The opposition he faced in Tigalate was comparatively easy to overcome, thanks to an intelligent campaign.

XXXIII.—Panoramic view of San Andrés y Sauces, Island of La Palma.

XXXIV.—The Blue Lagoon, in San Andrés y Sauces, Island of La Palma.

XXXV.—Partial view of the coastline and the Lighthouse of Barlovento, Island of La Palma.

XXXVI.—Partial view of Fuencaliente, Island of La Palma.

Before retiring to his winter quarters in Tazacorte, the princes Bentacaire, Atabara, Badiesta, Timeba, Badiesta of Garafía, and Atogmatoma —leaders of the tribes of Tedote, Tenagua, Adehayamen, Tagaragre, Galguen, and Hiscaguan respectively, submitted to Spanish supremacy. Left in sole opposition was the bold Tanausú.

3.—Attack on the Caldera and the Island's Surrender

The subjugation of the aforementioned districts foreshadowed the final conquest of the island. At the very centre of La Palma there stood the principality of Aceró, whose ruler, Tanausú, was one of the most courageous and enterprising Canarian warriors. Tanausú and his men had fortified their positions at Aceró (stronghold). The Spaniards were to call this place *Caldera de Taburiente* later on.

This bold prince offered his protection to those natives who had embraced his cause, and for a long time Lugo's efforts to evict him and his forces were in vain. Aceró was in truth impregnable because of its steep, rough slopes.

Lugo's first attempt was unsuccessful but the Spanish leader, undismayed, tried to penetrate through the Angustias ravine, where the Ajerjo stream ran, thinking that this was less impregnable. His native allies —for the subjugated tribes took part in this enterprise— guided him to a place known as *Paso del Capitán*, where the ravine narrowed. Carried on native shoulders, he crossed it with his officers. Tanausú, on knowing of his approach, quickly established a fortified position on one of the heights by the stream, and managed to stop the enemy's progress. Anxious to remove any hindrance, he made the old men, women and children hide in inaccessible caves.

Lugo, realizing it would be impossible to push his advance further, was on the point of giving up the undertaking when he devised and stratagem. Helped by one of the prince's kinsmen, he resolved to negotiate with Tanausú. But Tanausú refused to come to an agreement until the Spanish general had retreated with his troops to Aridane, where he would be ready to meet him. Lugo appeared to accept the terms stipulated and withdrew with some of his men. But he left a strong force at the pass, which was to cut off Tanausú's retreat when he marched to their appointment. Lugo did not await him where they had agreed, but met him at a place particularly propitious for an ambush. The Canarian prince went forward unsuspecting, but the Spanish general suddenly signalled his troops to attack. The battle that ensued was fought with equal courage on both sides, so much so that victory was uncertain until the Spaniards ambushed in the *Adamacansia* pass came to the help of their leader. Thus a formidable victory was finally won. This encounter on 3 May, 1493, was to put an end to the conquest of La Palma.

Alonso de Lugo did not prove particularly magnanimous towards his vanquished enemies:

«It is a pity that Lugo, who had effectively conquered the whole island except for the Aceró principality, in his haste to see the conquest of La Palma totally accomplished, besmirched his immaculate military career. He ought to have realized that Tanausú's days were numbered. The shameful deception he practised on the prince of the Caldera is one of the many unhappy episodes inseparable from any conquest.»

Tanausú, now a prisoner, was sent to Spain together with a vast number of captives; but the haughty Canarian prince, unwilling to see his country under a foreign yoke, committed suicide by refusing to eat.

We owe this paragraph on Tanausú to an illustrious Canarian writer who noted that:

«As soon as Tanausú lost sight of his native coast, he refused to take any food and consequently died of hunger during the journey. Thus, fate accorded a sublime, heroic death to the courageous King of Aceró. Captivity in his own island was impossible to bear, and once he left his native soil, he chose to die rather than live far from it —rather than become an unhappy prisoner at another king's court. His tomb must be sought in the ocean. The waves are the immense tombstones that cover his remains. But neither that infinite vault is spacious enough to write his name on it, nor can the vast tombstone hide his memory, which will live forever, and forever be venerated— keeping alive the glory of a prince who died for his country and its independence.»

The Spanish monarchs were overjoyed when they learned of Lugo's victory, and thereby appointed him governor of La Palma. Lugo sailed for Gran Canaria without further delay. He was anxious to start preparations for the conquest of Tenerife, which was to crown his highest ambitions.

His nephew, Juan Fernández de Lugo Señorino, remained in La Palma as Deputy Governor. He was entrusted with the task of bringing to a conclusion the pacification of the island, creating a council, and allotting the conquered lands.

4.—THE LANDING AT TENERIFE. EARLY SKIRMISHES

Not far from La Palma stands her fair neighbour, Tenerife, the white mountain, the Nivaria of ancient times, the land of perfumes according to Hannon's account, «an island created to ban melancholy from troubled spirits and offer them peace.»

> «... ilha querida,
> mimo do largo mar, cesta de flores
> esquecida na róta dos Phenicios.»
>
> (F. VARELA, *Song VII*)

> «Beloved island / This vast ocean's delight,
> basket of flowers / Forgotten on the route
> of the Proenicians.»

The name *Tenerife* in La Palma dialect is derived from *Tener* (mountain) and *if* (white). It means *white mountain*, a poetic allusion to the snow which often covers the Teide. Its early inhabitants, the Guanches, called it *Achinech*, and classical antiquity also knew it as the island of *Hell*.

This island, where the magnificent Guanche race lived, finally suffered the attack of the bold Spaniards on 1 May, 1494. The Spanish soldiers anchored off the beach of Azaña (where the capital of the island now stands). Lugo, their leader, had equipped 15 brigs which carried about 1,000 men at arms, 120 horses, and hundreds of Guanche auxiliaries from all the other islands.

On 4th May, the army left their quarters and made for the valley of La Laguna, but after an hour's march they were brought to a halt by the appearance of Guanche forces. Quebehi-Bencomo, the mencey of Tahoro, prepared to meet them, but first he harangued his men thus: «Behold those cowardly people, they daren't come any further for fear of us. I swear by the Echeyde and by the bones of my grandfather that they will have cause to remember me.»

Lugo sent an envoy to offer him an alliance similar in terms to those the princes of La Palma had accepted. After a conference where the mencey showed his extraordinary wisdom, they parted without having reached any agreement. Guillén Castellano acted as interpreter in these negotiations.

Bencomo retreated to his Tahoro domains and summoned all the other menceys, to discuss the course of war against their common enemy. This meeting was held at Arautapola (the present day Orotava Valley). Meanwhile, the Spanish General, on seeing the Guanches had chosen the path of war, returned to the Azaña encampment and had it fortified.

5.—THE GUANCHE PRINCES LEAGUE TOGETHER

On his arrival at Arautapola, Bencomo, after deliberating with the other menceys, asked to be appointed head of the league against the Spaniards. But uneasiness about Bencomo's marked superiority, to whom some attributed self-seeking aims, made the number of his allies dwindle.

The Guanche princes who joined forces with Bencomo against the Spaniards were: Acaymo, mencey of Tacoronte. He proved a faithful ally. This prince did not surrender until all was lost, and was brought before his adversary with a wounded leg and his spear dripping enemy blood. The mencey of Tegueste, Tegueste II, a brave tireless, soldier; Beneharo, mencey of Anaga, who was already an experienced warrior, for he had successfully opposed previous attacks from foreign adventurers before Lugo's arrival; Zebenzuí, who ruled over one of the smaller principalities in Tenerife. This illustrious barbarian embodied the heroic qualities of primitive courage and simplicity.

Those who refused to enter the league were: Atnoxa, mencey of Abona; Pelinor, mencey of Adeje; Rosmen, mencey of Daute; and Pelicar, mencey of Icod or Benicod. «These envious princes sadly weakened Bencomo's league against their common enemy, and thus brought about their nation's subjection, shamefully surrendering after neither fight nor glory.»

These princes who did not join Bencomo resolved to defend their own territories alone, with the exception of Añaterve of Guimar. He secretly favoured the Spaniards, to whom he proved a faithful friend, through the influence of a hermit called Antón.

6.—THE BATTLE OF ACENTEJO

Once Lugo realized the impossibility of persuading Bencomo to come to terms, and seeing that the latter was ready to present battle, he decided to march inland and seek him in his own domains. Lugo and his troops made for Tahoro in the spring of 1494. But Bencomo, learning in advance of Lugo's plans, sent word to his allies —the menceys of Tacoronte, Anaga, and Tegueste— whose states the Spanish troops had to cross, not to oppose a serious resistance which would warn Lugo of the dangers ahead.

The Spanish army arrived at Orotava without seeing traces of their enemy, but finding plenty of cattle grazing free in that fertile valley, which they seized. Then they proceeded towards the rich lowlands of La Laguna, encumbered by their booty.

Wily Bencomo, who had already positioned his troops, ordered his brother Tinguaro to lay in ambush with 300 chosen warriors at the Acentejo ravine. Meanwhile, the mencey of Tahoro with 3,000 men was following Lugo's steps, ready for battle.

Brave Tinguaro, showing the native mastery of this kind of warfare let the Spaniards proceed unmolested until they reached the ravine. Here the horses of the Spaniards proved useless. It was true that Spanish superiority was overwhelming. The Guanches, on top of having to fight on foot, also lacked cuirasses and other defence weapons —save for the small *tarjes* made of dragon-tree wood. They always fought naked, the *tamarco* wrapped round their left arm and holding the *banot*, a sort of spear, in their right hand. That any manner of opposition could be offered in such conditions was only due to the extraordinary nimbleness of those natives, their knowledge of the terrain, and their exceptional ability to fend off blows.

When the Spaniards arrived at the dangerous Acentejo ravine, the Guanches from above whistled to their cattle which, obedient to the well-known command, tried to break loose and stampede, thus causing a terrible havoc among the Spanish forces, who were vainly trying to assemble their ranks in presparation for battle.

The fight started in such unfavourable conditions for the conquering army that although Lugo and his men amply proved their courage and military discipline, they were totally defeated. They left 900 dead on the battlefield. The general himself was wounded in the mouth, thereby losing some teeth. His horse was killed too.

If Lugo managed to save his life, it was because of his having changed his red cloak by that of a soldier. The soldier was hotly pursued and slain by the Guanches, mistaking him for the General. With the help of some thirty Guanches from Guimar and mounting a horse Pedro Benítez procured him, Lugo managed to arrive at the Santa Cruz fortress.

The remaining forces were to suffer more disasters until they could finally make their way back to the almost deserted Azaña encampment. Only 200 soldiers survived the massacre.

The battle of Acentajo on May 31, 1594, was the most crushing Spanish defeat in the annals of the conquest. The death rate was also the highest. It was estimated that around 2,000 men were killed.

7.—THE ATTACK ON THE TOWER OF THE ENCAMPMENT. RETREAT TO GRAN CANARIA

Hardly had Alonso de Lugo recovered from the defeat at Acentajo when, on 1st. May, 400 Guanches led by Tayneto attacked the tower where he and his men had sought refuge. Tayneto lay siege to the fortress, but the Guanche leader was slain almost at once, and the Spanish forces put up a desperate fight, killing and wounding about 100 natives, thereby forcing the others to a retreat.

Lugo realized that, although he had won the day, he was in no position to withstand a further onslaught. He resolved to return to Gran Canaria, where he intended to equip a fresh expedition. He left a handful of men at the fortress and the rest sailed with him towards Gran Canaria on 8 June. They took with them some Guanches from Guimar, who were later sold as slaves in the Peninsula. However, when the Catholic Monarchs heard about this, immediately ordered their release for, in truth, these unfortunate captives were guilty of no crime, if we except the terrible one of having helped the Spanish against their own people.

8.—A FURTHER EXPEDITION AGAINST THE GUANCHES. BATTLE OF LA LAGUNA

Fernández de Lugo and all the other noblemen who accompanied him to Tenerife had invested the greater part of their fortunes in the enterprise. Now, they engaged the Genoese merchants, Palomar, Angelote, Blanco, and Viña to furnish all that would be needed in a long campaign. Moreover, Lugo and the other noblemen had persuaded Don Juan Guzmán, Duke of Medina Sidonia, to take part in the enterprise. This powerful gentleman raised an impressive army —600 infantrymen and 50 horse. They set sail from San Lúcar de Barrameda under Colonel Bartolomé de Estupiáñez, a nobleman belonging to one of the most important families in Jerez, and under Captain Diego de Mesa, the son of the master of the garrison at Jimena. The expedition arrived at the Canaries in October.

Lugo had meanwhile raised a fair number of troops in Gran Canaria; and he could also count on several noblemen, who were personal friends of his. Among them was Lope Hernández de la Guerra, one of the conquerors of that island, whose good sense and military prowess were to prove invaluable.

This army arrived at Santa Cruz on 2 November, 1494, ready to conquer the island or die in the enterprise. Their banners were the pennant given by Ferdinand and Isabella to Lugo —which can now be seen at the La Laguna Townhall— the standard of the Count of Niebla, their patron, and that of the Duke of Medina Sidonia. They set up camp near the Azaña fortress, and thus started the second and final campaign. Lugo's forces at the time amounted to 1,100 infantrymen and 70 horse.

When Bencomo learned of their arrival, he established his headquarters at La Laguna de Aguere, where the other chieftains and their respective forces soon assembled. There, on November 13, Guanches and Spaniards met in pitched battle.

Historians have no doubt exaggerated the outcome of this battle. According to them, the Spanish forces only lost forty five men whereas natives losses amounted to no less than 1,700 dead.

As Unamuno rightly pointed out: «Our chroniclers were never good at statistics. Their estimates were based on what they thought could be an approximate number.»

Bencomo and Acaymo had to retreat, seriously wounded. Tinguaro was killed by a cavalry soldier. He had been wounded soon after the battle started, but in spite of this, he bravely fought against seven cavalry soldiers brandishing a halberd he had won at Acentajo. He was wounded again, and unable to defend himself, vainly begged for mercy, but Martín Buen-Día felled him with a stroke of his spear. The prince had cried: «Do not kill the noble brother of King Bencomo, who is ready to become your prisoner!» But the Spanish soldier, deaf to his supplications, pierced his breast with a second, mighty thrust. Tinguaro's head was stuck on a pike as a fearful warning to the natives.

This battle, which took place on 14 November, 1494, was to seal the fate of the island.

The Spanish, eager to commemorate their victory, erected a cross at the gates of La Laguna —a cross now known as the *Cruz de Piedra* (Stone Cross). They also built a small hermitage dedicated to Our Lady of Grace.

9.—FURTHER PROGRESS OF THE CONQUERING ARMY. PLAGUE DECIMATES THE GUANCHES

The battle of La Laguna was to have a terrible aftermath. The Guanches suffered from a deadly plague, which was probably due to the great number of unburied bodies left on the battlefield after Aguere. This plague spread all over the island and prevented further Guanche attacks.

On 31 January, 1495, a troop of 500 Spanish soldiers on a reconnaisance mission in La Laguna found nothing but corpses. Death seemed to have silenced the valleys of Tejina and Tegueste, which had once been bustling with life. But, in spite of this awful calamity, the Guanches had such a horror of slavery that when a group of Spanish soldiers found a dying old man and his three sons in a cave, this man killed himself with his javelin, rather than be captured alive.

These 500 men, led by the Captains Trujillo and Castillo, had seized a herd of goat and were about to return to camp when they were suddenly attacked at the Peñuelas Pass by 1,200 warriors under Zebensuí and Tegueste. The Spaniards, however, put them to flight after having lost only twelve men. The Guanches left ninety men on the battlefield but Captain Castillo, in hot pursuit of Zebensuí, was captured after his horse was slain. He was sent to Araurápola and there he fell in love with the fair Dácil, Bencomo's daughter, who interceded with the mencey on behalf of the prisoner. Thanks to her entreaties, he was set free without ransom.

10.—THE FEAT OF THE TWELVE SOLDIERS

There is in the annals of the conquest a remarkable exploit, known as the feat of *the twelve dauntless soldiers.* Alonso de Lugo had remained at Azaña, unwilling to let his men invade those valleys where plague spread. But twelve officers set forth carrying out several bold raids. They proceeded as far as Ygueste and entered Taganana, where they seized seven shepherds and a fair amount of cattle. On their way back themselves surrounded by 200 islanders led by Beneharo. The Canarian chieftain thus came face to face with these *twelve dauntless soldiers*, who did not cower before an enemy far superior in number.

The Spaniards closed the ranks and one of them, called Rodrigo Barrios, cried: «It is better for you to surrender now, for we have already made our reckoning, and we know exactly how many heads will be cut off by each of us!» Beneharo was greatly impressed by such courage and ordered his men to let them go their way unmolested. But one the soldiers, Juan de Llarena, eager to win his little parcel of glory, urged his comrades to put up a fight. They attacked the Guanches sword in hand, after firing their muskets and crossbows. Some of the natives were wounded and the rest put to flight. Bold Beneharo, wounded and forsaken by his men, threw himself over a cliff to avoid falling in the hands of his enemies. And thus, those twelve men, whom Viera called *The Twelve Peers of Our Conquest*, triumphantly arrived at the Santa Cruz encampment, after having performed one of the most stupendous feats in the conquest of the Canaries.

11.—FOOD SHORTAGE AT THE SPANISH CAMP. LOPE HERNÁNDEZ DE LA GUERRA'S GENEROUS GESTURE

Life at the Spanish camp proved more and more difficult as the days passed. The small raids made did not yield enough victuals. Food shortage grew daily and so desperate was the situation that many officers thought the troops should be withdrawn from the island, until food supply could be secured by the conquest of further lands. But Lugo remained undaunted and summoned the other leaders of the expedition, making clear to them his firm resolution to be the first in sharing both hardships and dangers rather than renounce the glorious enterprise.

The alternative Lugo's words offered to his weary men was a terrible one. The solemn silence following his speech was in itself an answer —the courageous acceptance of the hardships ahead. Then, Lope Hernández de la Guerra spoke, bringing new hope to his comrades. He was to sell two sugar mills in order to pay for the victuals so desperately needed. This was indeed a lofty gesture, for it meant sacrificing all that he possessed.

Hernández de la Guerra, anxious to bring back the relief he had offered, left at once for Gran Canaria where he sold his possessions obtaining 2,000 *doblas* for them. This he used to pay the provisions. When he returned to Santa Cruz, the scarcity of food was such that a soldiers' daily ration consisted of just a handful of cooked barley.

12.—THE SECOND BATTLE OF ACENTEJO

Lope Hernández de la Guerra's arrival bringing the much needed victuals raised the spirits of the conquering troops. Lugo took advantage of this happier mood to launch an attack on the last Guanche stronghold.

On the twenty-fourth of December, the army set forth towards the Acentejo ravine, where they encamped once more. The next day, the battle was fought.

The Guanches were by now ready to risk everything. Both armies once again met near the Acentajo ravine —almost at the very spot where the previous encounter had taken place. Bencomo led 5,000 Guanches, whom he divided into two units, one under his own command and the other under that of Acaymo. Lugo also divided his forces in a similar way, sharing the command with Lope Hernández de la Guerra.

After five hours of fierce fighting, which cost the natives countless lives, Bencomo and Acaymo were finally seriously wounded and their troops, deprived of their leaders, panicked. The old mencey of Tahoro, in a desperate attempt to avoid utter defeat, signalled his troops to retreat and withdrew behind Barranco Hondo, from where they were to march back to Arautapola. Seeing their enemies in full flight, the Spaniards burst into cheerful shouts of «Victory!», and this word, repeated a thousand times, became the name of the village which was later built on the very spot of the battle.

This outstanding triumph cost the Spanish army only sixty four lives, as compared to the more than 2,000 men that the Guanches lost. Among the Guanches slain was Badeñol, the brother of Acaymo, who was killed by Pedro Benítez de Lugo.

13.—THE SPANIARDS INVADE THE VALLEY OF ARAUTAPOLA AND TENERIFE IS FINALLY CONQUERED

Alonso Fernández de Lugo could well have continued his campaign after such a sweeping victory, but he wisely retreated to the Azaña encampment, until the rainy season was over and the reinforcements sent from Spain by the Duke of Medina Sidonia had arrived. Thus, he made no further move until the first of July, when he once more set forth with his troops and entered the valley of Arautapola, where Bencomo had entrenched his forces. Bencomo, on the other hand, after changing the position of his army, considered at lenght the likely outcome of the new encounter and weighed his own scanty possibilities of success. He finally decided that surrender was best so as not to incur more senseless bloodshed. Lugo was overjoyed when he heard of this decision, for thus the long awaited hour of total victory had arrived.

Alonso Fernández de Lugo met the native chieftain before his tent, surrounded by all his officers. The mencey of Tahoro walked slowly up to him, with an expression of infinite sorrow upon his face and eyes clouded with the pain of a lacerated heart. His tremulous voice when paking homage to Lugo, though showing unabated courage, could not mask the torment of a soul forced by an adverse fate to renounce its most cherished ideals. He approached the general, took his hands and addressed him in a memorable speech, which was translated at once by an interpreter:

«You are a courageous man, and we regret having fought you so bitterly, though we have always regarded you as our cruellest enemy. But we now want to accept the terms you have offered us in the past. We are ready to accept the Catholic King and Queen as our rulers and thus we will pay them homage and give them this island, which we inherited from the great Tinerfe, our grandfather. We want to be baptized, but you must swear by all that you hold dear that neither we nor our children will ever become slaves, and that we will enjoy that freedom which is so dear to us and for which we have amply paid with our blood.»

Lugo was deeply moved by these words. He had a missal brought, over which he swore to faithfully keep his promise. Unfortunately, notwithstanding that first and commendable magnanimity, Lugo was later to indulge in the base complacency of transporting Bencomo and most of the other Guanche princes to Spain. The aged mencey of Tahoro was taken from town to town and brought before the Pope and the Venetian Dux.

On September 29, 1496, the whole island was at last completely pacified and a solemn *Te Deum* was sung.

The poet Viana put the following lines in Bencomo's mouth, upon surrendering:

> Cristiano quiero ser, no más batalla,
> Cese el peligro y daño de la guerra,
> Que no puede Nivaria sustentalla
> Contra el de España, do el valor se encierra;
> La tierra suya al cabo ha de ganalla,
> Y quiero yo rendir corona y tierra,
> Y acabe de Bencomo la memoria,
> Pues se acabó de rey el cetro y gloria.
> Mas! Ay! Querida patria, que he de veros
> Sin libertad sujeta y gobernada
> Con otras leyes y con otros fueros.
> O por mejor decir tiranizada!
> Quién lo podrá sufrir? Mas quien valeros.
> Si Dios lo ordena así, si Dios le agrada
> Y el gran poder de España al vuestro escede?
> Que la ayuda de Dios todo lo puede.

(VIANA, *Chapter 15*)

I will become a Christian, let the battle cease / The dangers and evils of war must stop / For Nivaria can no longer sustain it / Against this Spaniard, full of courage; / His native country has finally won it, / and I want to surrender crown and land, / and may thus end the memory of Bencomo, / as the sceptre and the glory of this king has ended / But alas! dear land, that I must see you / Deprived of freedom and ruled / By alien laws and alien customs. / Or rather, tyrannized! / Who will be able to bear it? But who could help you? / If this be God's will, and if this does please Him / And Spain's mighty power yours surpasses? / For with God's help nothing is impossible.

Thus ended the conquest of the Canary Islands, after ninety two years of struggle with the bold islanders winning more than twenty battles. Their patriotism and love of freedom were subjected to grievous trials, during more than a century of ceaseless turmoil. The war declared upon them was a fight to the death, which they courageously accepted. But their strenght, their cunning, their many stratagems and their marvellous nimbleness were of no avail against the weapons of the Spanish. Sublime heroism and the most tenacious opposition were vanquished in such an unequal encounter.

Hundreds of bold warriors, relentlessly pursued, died in their impregnable strongholds —sacrified to that freedom which they had been unable to preserve. The others gradually mixed with the conquering race until they became only one nation.

The Catholic Monarchs gave the archipelago such an autonomous municipal régime that it was called republican. The Adelantados were to maintain national unity, and these officials established their quarters at San Cristóbal de La Laguna.

The conquest of the Canaries opened the American route to adventurers, and events similar to those we have just narrated were to take place in the New World, though in far less dramatic circumstances.

The heroic nation defeated was, however, not totally annihilated, as some chroniclers maintain. From the accounts left by historians after the war of conquest had come to an end, it becomes clear that the Canary Islands had scarcely lost 20 per cent of their total population, estimated in more than 100,000 people.

A significant fact, concerning the survival of the primitive race under Spanish rule, may be found in the report submitted by the bailiff of Las Palmas, Fernando de Porras, towards the end of the fifteenth century. He informed the council that the island had far too many free natives, whose behaviour was extremely suspicious.

We may thus positively assert, together with those anthropologists who have studied the history of the Canaries prior to the conquest, that the native race, with the Guanches as the most typical representatives, did certainly survive under Spanish administration. This race increased down the generations, whether through mixed marriages or remaining pure, and thus it preserved its original characteristics under the influence of hereditary laws.

The fusion of the two races, started during the war of conquest which lasted for ninety four years, almost for the whole of the fifteenth century (1402 - 1496), was to increase greatly after the islands were pacified.

XXXVII.—A typical scene, with the Montaña del Fuego (Fire Mountain) in the background, Lanzarote.

XXXVIII.—The Inferno de Timanfaya, inside this mound temperature rises above 400° C., Lanzarote.

XXXIX.—Panoramic view of Puerto Rosario, capital of Fuerteventura.

XL.—Montaña del Fuego (Fire Mountain). Lanzarote.

CHAPTER XI

The Colonizations of the Islands; Contribution of the Canaries to the Conquest and Colonization of America

    A.—Colonization of the Canary Islands Under the Patronage of the Spanish Monarchs

    B.—Canarian contribution to the Conquest and Colonization of America

A.—The Colonization of the Canary Islands Under the Patronage of the Spanish Monarchs

At the time of the conquest, various pressures led to the subjection of the native tribes, but the law established by the conquerors was far from cruel. It is true that many outrageous violations of human rights took place during the war that culminated in the conquest of the islands, but the Catholic Monarchs promptly gave strict orders to curtail such abuses.

As soon as the conquest was accomplished, the natives actually enjoyed the same rights as other Spanish subjects, as stipulated in the chart drawn at San Cristóbal de La Laguna in 1514.

That the native race was not considered an inferior one is clearly shown by the high number of mixed marriages that took place. The romance between Dácil and Captain Gonzalo del Castillo, which was to inspire Lope de Vega's famous play «the Guanches of Tenerife and the Conquest of the Canaries», may be considered the poetic symbol of an important social phenomenon: the brotherhood of two races. It also demonstrated how the Spaniards accepted the Guanches as their equals, even before this primitive race had forgotten its habits and customs and had learned those of the new civilization.

The Spanish Kings were particularly eager to allot the lands equitably. The royal warrant given on 20 January, 1487, by which the Catholic Monarchs accepted the distribution of lands and water made by General Pedro de Vera, included the following clause: «If any member or members of the community living in the aforesaid island of Gran Canaria, were wronged because of this partition, they should be heard and then their wrongs amended according to what the law provides in these cases.»

In those islands where the Crown had direct intervention, the actions taken were animated by the highest aims. The Spanish Kings never allowed the natives to become slaves, and it was always attempted to deal justly with them. If under the rule of the monarchs the natives were sometimes transported as slaves, Espinosa categorically asserted that: «The Kings immediately ordered their release and granted them the right to live as free men.»

Likewise, the Spanish church was always strongly opposed to slavery. The churchmen protected the natives against the Portuguese, who often captured the Canarians, either through false promises or by violence, and took them to the island of Madeira where they were to till the soil. when Fray Fernando Calvetos was appointed Bishop of Rubicón in Lanzarote in 1431, he ardently strove to abolish this inhuman trade and strictly forbade the sale of any of the islanders, whether baptized or not. But on realizing that his spiritual threats were to no avail, he brought the case before the Holy See and Pope Eugene the IV issued a bull, dated 25 October, 1434, which read: «On behalf of the new converts in the Canaries, we forbid, under the gravest bans, the ill treatment and the subjection to slavery of any of these islanders, for these horrible cruelties only serve to make them abhor Christianity.»

In the bull sent to Don Diego López de Illescas, Bishop of Rubicón, by Pius II, drawn at Petreoli on 9 October, 1462, the zeal of this prelate was highly praised, for López de Illescas frequently visited those heathen islands accompanied by other priests, in order to peacefully convert them.

Thus did the Spanish church and the bishops of the Canaries act and this general attitude of Christian charity was confirmed by Paul III, urged by Cardinal Tavera, Archbishop of Toledo, in a papal brief dated in 1537 by which he excommunicated «latae sententiae» all those who reduced to slavery or deprived those «Indians» of their belongings, even if they had not been baptized.

Indeed a rapid and thorough amalgamation of the two races took place, through the friendship sprung between the conquered and their conquerors, through mixed marriages, and also, through the genuine admiration the Spaniards felt for the splendid virtues of the Canarians. This may be said to be a unique example in the history of colonization and conquest.

B.—CANARIAN CONTRIBUTION TO THE CONQUEST AND COLONIZATION OF AMERICA

The identity achieved between the native spirit and that of the conquering race is proved by the institution of military levies. Philip II withdrew the peninsular troops from the Canaries and replaced them with native soldiers, and by a royal warrant issued on 25 January, 1598, he instituted the provincial militia by which all the able men were drafted into the army.

The Canarians not only fought in the islands for their own protection, but they also played a key role in all Spanish military enterprises. They heroically participated in the African Wars; they generously sent their own people to colonize America. Canarians were also found in Flemish battlefields and in Extremadura, Portugal, and Cataluna, whenever the Spanish crown needed her faithful sons. And, finally, they were to shed their blood in the war of Succession and in the War of Independence.

Many feats were performed by the Canarians in the conquest and colonization of America —feats that we will now briefly survey.

Herrera in his *Décadas* and Juan de Castellanos in *Elegías de Varones Ilustres de Indias*, mentioned Agustín Delgado, Jerónimo de Hortal's lieutenant, praising his exploits at Paria. Castellanos also spoke about Antón del Guante and Gaspar de Santa Fé, who took part in Hortal's expedition and amply proved their courage. Juan el Canario was also mentioned as a Canarian who won great renown at the Hispaniola or Santo Domingo island. And one must not forget Luis Perdomo, conqueror of Paria and the hero of Puerto Rico.

Pedro Fernández de Lugo, the second Adelantado de Canarias, ruled the province of Santa María by virtue of an agreement signed by the Emperor in 1535. He was set upon conquering more territories for the Spanish Crown through the subjection of the inland districts. According to Viera, it was a measure of his prowess that his name was given to a pass, the «Paso del Adelantado», and this same historian adds that he gave the name of Santa Marta to the vast province under his rule in memory of Santa Marta de Ortigueira, a village in Galicia from here his family came.

Nor must we forget, among the Canarian conquerors in the New World, Juan de Santa Cruz, the Adelantado's lieutenant and governor of Cartagena de Indias, to whom Santa Cruz de Nompox owes its name, nor Don Miguel and Don Alonso López, sons of Lope Daya Gallego, one of the conquerors of Tenerife, who participated in the conquest of Río de la Plata, together with Pedro Benítez and Francisco Benítez.

Almost every expedition sent to America took its share of victuals, soldiers, and sailors when it touched at the Canaries.

Undoubtedly, Columbus must have recruited men the many times he put in at the Canaries. It seems highly probable that, the first time he stopped there to repair the *Pinta*'s helm, he also increased the number of his crew with some experienced seamen, well used to sailing the stormy seas and, according to a distinguished Canarian writer, the first man to sight the New Continent was one of those islanders.

Francisco Montejo was to land in the Canaries in 1526 on his way to America, where he conquered Yucatán, and there he recruited a good number of men who embarked on board a Canarian vessel. On their arrival at Veracruz, they joined Hernán Cortés's army and there participated in the last glorious stage of the conquest of Nueva España.

In the expedition prepared by Don Pedro Fernández de Lugo, for the conquest of Tierra Firme, of the 1,700 or 1,800 men participating in it, almost half of them were Canarians. Among them were: «many of his own kin and other noblemen and honest citizens from Tenerife, La Palma, and the other islands.» These were the ones who accompanied him in his exploration of the Río Grande or Magdalena, and in the conquest of the New Kingdom of Granada. The towns of Tenerife and Palma are proofs of the Canarian contribution in peopling the New Kingdom.

We also find Canarians in the colonization of the Hispaniola island. When the King granted a license of trade with America, it was established that in 1678, 50 Canarian families, numbering at least five persons each, should be taken to the Hispaniola or Santo Domingo island. In 1685, an expedition integrated by peasants and workmen left the port of Santa Cruz de Tenerife bound for that island, where they set up the colony of San Carlos de Tenerife.

Cuba, Havana, Vuelta de Abajo, Matanzas, Sagua, San Fernando, San Carlos de Nuevitas, and Guantánamo were also to have a considerable amount of Canarian population.

According to the Venezuelan writer Manuel María Marrero, two ships —«Nuestra Señora de la Soledad» and the «Santiago», sailed from Tenerife with seventy Canarian families on board. They were taken to Florida, where they established the San Agustín colony.

When in 1778 the colonization of Lousiana was attempted, the Canaries likewise sent many of their men. It is estimated that more than 4,000 of them settled there.

The natives of the islands were the first to work the fertile Venezuelan soil and took an important part in the development of the cities of Caracas, Valencia, La Victoria, Cumaná, Barquisimeto, and Coro. The Candelaria Square, in Caracas, was, about the middle of the xviii century, the centre of a flourishing Canarian colony. The islanders had erected there a church in honour of the Virgin of Candelaria, who had miraculously appeared before the conquest and was fervently venerated in the Archipelago.

The Candelarian Islands in the Gulf of Mexico, the village of Gomera in Guatemala, and those of Realejo in Nicaragua and Candelaria in Paraguay, clearly show by their names the Canarian origin of their first settlers.

After this initial stage, the attraction the New World held for the islanders did not wane, and thus, quite a number of Canarian families have immigrated there, especially in those countries of Spanish origins.

It would take us too much time to record the many instances in which the Canarians have willingly left their homes to serve their Mother Country. Canarian forces came to the Peninsula in 1809 to fight for Spanish independence, and the surnames of some of the officers show that they belonged to the oldest families in the island: Oramas, Perdomo, Massieu, and Bravo de Laguna. Sebastián Pérez, father of the novelist Pérez Galdós, served as lieutenant in the Canarian battalion which was sent to the Peninsula under Juan María de León y Romero.

Among the most remarkable events in the history of these islands was the utter defeat inflicted upon Sir Francis Drake, and also upon the Dutch pirate Van der Doez. Nor must we forget one of the most splendid pages in the history of the Canaries, namely, Sir Horace Nelson's attack on Tenerife on 25 July, 1797. Nelson, the hero of Aboukir Bay and Trafalgar, the greatest naval genius of his age, was in command of the «Emerald», the «Theseus», the «Mary-Emerald», the «Horse-Mare», the «Thunderbolt», and the «Terpsichore», which was the first to open fire against the town's fortifications. Shortly afterwards, the «Vixen», an English cutter, sank and her captain, together with 57 members of the crew, were drowned. Undaunted, the British forces disembarked, but the Spanish guns were fired upon them incessantly and they had to retreat to their ships. They left 226 dead behind, among them Captain Bowen, of the «Terpsichore», and carried 123 wounded men on board.

It was at his encounter that Nelson lost his right arm. In the Municipal Museum at Santa Cruz de Tenerife, visitors may see the «Tigre», the cannon which wounded Nelson, and whoever ventures to go as far as La Cuesta, between Santa Cruz and La Laguna, will be shown the castle from where this cannon was fired. Moreover, in the parish church of La Concepción, at Santa Cruz de Tenerife, are preserved the

English banners seized on that occasion. Commander Troubridge, captain of the «Culloden», and the man under whom the landing forces were placed, told how, once the battle was over and before his men went on board, they were offered plenty of food and wine and were pleasantly entertained by the Canarians. This anecdote is but another proof of the true nobility of the islanders, who were ready to befriend their enemies.

The spiritual bonds between the Archipelago and the Peninsula are today as firm as ever. These ties of patriotism and affection may be called indissoluble.

Though a veritable invasion from other countries has recently taken place, due to the well-known beauty of the Fortunate Islands and their splendid climate, such a display of power and luxury —for the foreign invasion has indeed added more wealth to these islands— has not dazzled the Canarians, nor has it weakened their steadfast devotion to their Mother Country.

APPENDICES

I.—Atlantis in Plato's Works
II.—The Tiahuanaco Ruins

APPENDICES

I.—ATLANTIS IN PLATO'S WORKS

In Plato's *Timaeus*, Critias gives the following account: Solon told us that there (among the Egyptians of the Delta) he had aquired high renown and that once, when he chanced to ask several of the most learned priests about ancient times, he realized that neither he nor any other Greek for that matter, knew anything about it.

Solon had first spoken about what the Greeks knew of earliest antiquity: the first man, Foroneus, and Deucalion's flood.

«But one of the priests, a very old man, told him: Solon, Solon, you Greeks will always be like children, a Greek never ages! On hearing this, Solon asked: What do you mean by those words? And the priest answered: You are so young because you only care about the soul and in it you will not find any ancient wisdom, sprung from some old tradition, nor any science which time has ripened.

»And the reason for it is that men have been anihilated and will be so again, in various differents ways. There is a story among the Greeks that narrates the fate of Phaeton, son of Helios, who, having demanded of his father to let him drive the Sun's chariot for one day, was incapable to guide the chariot, and heaven and earth were threatened with a universal conflagration when Jupiter struck the driver with one of his thunderbolts. This, of course, is a beautiful legend but there is a true event behind it. Sometimes the heavenly bodies are deviated from their usual orbits around the earth. Thus, at very wide intervals, everything upon the Earth is destroyed by fire, and those living in the mountains and other high places or in dry climates are easier victims than those who dwell near the sea or a river. But we are spared such a fate by the

181

Nile, our benefactor in so many other instances, which then floods our lands. On the other hand, when the gods purify the Earth by means of water and submerge it, only the shepherds in the mountains are safe. But in this country, the waters never flow from the heights towards the plains, neither then nor on any other occasion, for they, by a natural prenomenon, gush forth from underground. Maybe it is because of this that here we have preserved the most ancient traditions. But the truth is that in those places where the climate is neither excessively cold nor unbearably hot, there will always be settlers. Thus, whether it be in your country or in ours, if something great or beautiful has been achieved, it has been recorded here from remotest antiquity, in our temples. However, this is not so in your case or in that of the other nations, because as soon as you have reached stability and organization, and have learned about writing and all those matters necessary to the welfare of the State, the rains, like a heavenly disease, fall and drown all but the ignorant and the unlettered. This happens at regular intervals and then you become young once again, losing all memory of what had happened here, or even in your own nation, in times past. In truth, my dear Solon, those genealogies you were quoting a short while ago or, at least, what you have just told me about your country's history, is but a fairy tale. And above all, you only speak about one flood, though there have been many more before that one.

»The priest then added: It is written in our records that your city vanquished, once upon a time, an insolent power who was invading the whole of Europe and Asia and whose homeland was at the far end of the Atlantic Ocean. Because at that time it was impossible to cross that sea. There stood an island facing that passage which you call the Pillars of Hercules. This island was bigger than Libya and Asia together. Travellers in those days could go from that island to the other islands, and from them they could cross to that continent which stood on the other side of that sea, which in truth merited its name. On one side of that strait of which we are speaking, it seems that there was only a roads with a very narrow access and on the other side stood the open seas, thus, the land that surrounded it could properly be called a continent. Besides, this empire ruled over Libyan territory as far as Egypt, and over Europe as far as the Tyrrhenian Sea. Once this power had achieved an enormous strenght, it attempted to conquer both your territory and ours, and also all those that lie this side of the strait. It was then, dear Solon, that your city's heroism and energy set us a memorable example, for she far exceeded all others in bravery and military prowess. Placed at first at the head of all the Hellenic people, later on by herself due to sheer force of circumstances, deserted by all when in the greatest peril, she secured the victory defeating the invaders and rescuing from slavery those who had never been slaves. She generously released all the other nations including ourselves who live in the inner region of the Pillars of Hercules. But as time went by, terrible earthquakes and cataclysms supervened. In just one day and one night your army was buried underground and it was then also that the island of Atlantis was covered by the sea and disappeared, which is the reason why, even today, that ocean is difficult to sail and remains unexplored. Because the submerged island is a terrible danger to seamen.»

We find in *Critias* a fuller narrative, where some details are added to the brief account given in *Timaeus:*

«The only survivors were those who dwelt on the mountains, who did not know how to write. They, and their descendants for many generations, lacked the usual comforts and had to devote all their energies and intelligence to satisfying their physical needs. Thus, it is not surprising that they forgot what had happened in ancient times. This, moreover, explains why only the names of our distant ancestors have reached us, while their deeds have been forgotten.

»For many generations and for as long as divine inspiration guided their steps, the kings abided by the law were faithful to the divine principle from which they descended. Their troughts were illuminated by wisdom and truth and all their actions were prompted by kindness and reason. They only cared about true virtues despising earthly splendour; their gold and their wealth were but a burden to them and they were never dazzled by vast richesses. They never lost the command of their passions and always followed the straight path. Good judgement and experience taught them that wealth increased through mutual love and virtue, whereas an exaggerated worry over it only entailed its diminution and also that of virtue. Thanks to this belief and to the divine presence within them, all that opulence to which we have referred grew incessantly. But when divine inspiration started to disappear, due to the constant contact with human principles, they were unable to wisely accept their prosperity and they fell prey to the worst vices. Wise men despised them for thus losing their most precious possession. On the other hand, those who were unable to realize which way of life was the one conducive to real happiness, hailed them as the most perfect and fortunate people on earth, though now they were filled with boundless greed and drunk with power. Then, the King of the Heavens, Zeus, who abides by the law and who had heard all about their misdeeds, saw that this race, who had at first been so excellently good, would sink into utter corruption. He resolved to punish them and thus make them reflect on their folly so that they would follow the right path once again. To that purpose, he assembled all the other gods in his noble palace, which stands at the heart of the Universe and from where he could forsee all future events. Once the gods were there, he told them...»

And here ends the narrative in *Critias*.

XLI.—The House of the Colonels, with rich baroque decorations. Fuerteventura.

XLII.—Slag and lava land which the native peasants turn into fertile orchards. Lanzarote.

XLIII.—Plato. Marble bust (Vatican Museum).

XLIV.—Monolith called «El Fraile» (The Friar), at the Tihuanaco ruins.

II.—THE TIAHUANACO RUINS

The Tiahuanaco ruins, among the oldest primitive remains to be found in South America, stand at about twenty kilometres from the Titicaca Lake in the Andes. These ruins are the only evidence left of a civilization which was extinct even before the Incas. According to one legend, those stones were once magnificent palaces built by a race of giants.

Squier maintains that the Tiahuanaco stones are cut with such perfection that their equals are to be found nowhere else. According to Posnansky, those buildings were made of materials taken from the Tapia hill, a spent volcano in the Junguyo isthmus, where the Copacabana peninsula joins the Continent. It is believed that molten lava from the erupting volcano was used in the construction. It must have been carried along channels to the foot of the mountain and there moulded by a process similar to that employed with molten iron. On the other hand, there are moulds at Tiahuanaco which show clear signs of having been used to cast idols.

Geologically, the blocks of stone which were used to build Tiahuanaco are of very hard trachite, basalt, slate, granite, porphyry, and red clay. Thus, volcanic stone was used to erect these ruins.

H. S. Bellamy in his magnificent book entitled *Built before the Flood —the Problem of Tiahuanaco* pointed out that: the Tiahuanaco ruins offer unique characteristics, not to be found anywhere else. The primitive Andean civilization bears no resemblance to any later cultures, and its peculiarities cannot be understood unless we date it back to an infinitely remote period.

The faces of the colossal statues there are witness to the degree of perfection that culture achieved. They clearly suggest that Tiahuanaco was one of the starting points in the history of mankind.

A calendar, carved on stone in a portico more than three metres in height and breadth, is a clear proof of the intellectual superiority of that race. This portico was half buried in dry slime, split in two due to a crack at the top, but held together by stones weighing more than ten tons. Ponansky, a veteran in Bolivian archeological studies, was the first to realize that it was in fact a calendar and was thus able to identify the signs representing the solstices and equinoxes. A German scientist, Kiss, after conducting a prolonged research there in 1928 and 1929, deciphered those connected with months and weeks. Ashton, an English scholar, was to make a compilation in 1949 of all the facts known about that system, thus showing how it worked.

According to some archeologists, the Tiahuanaco calendar is better than ours. This does not mean that it is more perfect than the one our astronomers could devise if asked to do so; but it is far superior to the current one. We cannot, of course, assert that the Tiahuanaco astronomers were more learned than ours, for we know hardly anything about them. But the fact remains that the men for whom they designed the calendar were more fortunate than we are.

Neither the Greeks nor the Hindus nor even the Egyptians could have been able to devise such a calendar. But pride in the scientific discoveries made in the nineteenth and twentieth centuries has led us to believe in our superiority over the Andean civilization of the Tertiary Period. Moreover, where art is concerned, they far excelled our achievements, in my opinion, and so did the Egyptians. Europe never produced, not even during the Italian Renaissance, a masterpiece such as the face of the colossal statue the Spaniards baptized *The Friar*. There emanates from those features a sort of supreme kindness, of supreme wisdom —thus the impression left upon our hearts by the statue is one of absolute harmony. The stylized hands and feet establish a delicate balance which has in itself not only an artistic but a moral quality. A sense of peacefulness and serenity seems to flow from that magnificent monolith.

Bellamy writes: «The carved heads show high brows, open countenances, bold profiles, and vigorous jaws. There is a head in particular —the head of some high dignitary in all probability, as it wears a sort of official headdres— that is truly unforgettable. It seems about to escape the stone on which it is carved, for it has been left unfinished, as if the sculptor had impatiently dropped his chisel, in the knowledge that it would live forever.»

BIBLIOGRAPHY

SELECTED BIBLIOGRAPHY

The following is a short list of works dealing with the Canaries which may be read to supplement the present book. Chief among our suggestions for further reading is Fray Alonso de Espinosa's *History*. Espinosa, having arrived in the Canaries when the generation of the conquest had but recently disappeared, could, with difficulty, collect reliable information about the primitive inhabitants of the islands. He has been the main source of later writers, who have not added much to what the illustrious Dominican friar had already written. Some of the works cited below have also been consulted when writing the present book.

ABREU GALINDO, Fray Juan de: *Historia de la Conquista de las Islas Canarias*, 1632. Reprinted at Santa Cruz de Tenerife. Valentín Sanz Press, 1940.

ALFONSO, Leoncio: *Esquema de Geografía Física de las Islas Canarias.* La Laguna de Tenerife, 1953.

ALVAREZ CRUZ, Luis: *Retablo Isleño*. Goya ed. Santa Cruz de Tenerife, 1941.

ALVAREZ DELGADO, Juan: *Ensayo de Filología Tinerfeña*. Instituto de Estudios Canarios. La Laguna, 1945.

— *Las Islas Afortunadas en Plinio*, Revista de Historia, XI, 1945. La Laguna-Tenerife.

BAILLY, Jean Silvain: *Histoire de l'Astronomie*, Paris, 1775-87.
— *Lettres sur l'Atlantide de Platon et l'ancienne Historia de l'Asie*, London 1778.

BALLESTEROS Y BERETTA, Antonio: *Historia de América y de los Pueblos Americanos*, Vol. III. Barcelona-Salvat ed. Hispanoamericana, 1936-1955.

BELLAMY, H. S.: *A Life History of Earth*. Faber, London, 1951.
— *The Book of Revelation is History*. Faber, London, 1942.

Berthelot and Weebs: *Histoire Naturelle des Yles Canaries.* Paris, 1836-1850.

Bessmertny, Alexandre: *L'Atlantide Exposé des Hypotheses Relations a l'enigme de l'Atlantide.* Translated by F. Gidon. Paris. Payot, 1935.

Bory de St. Vincent: *Ideas Generales Sobre las Islas Canarias.* Santa Cruz de Tenerife, 1847.

Bute, Marquis of: *Of the Ancient Language of the Natives of Tenerife.* London, 1891.

Castillo Ruiz de Vergara, Pedro Agustín: *Descripción Histórica y Geográfica de las Islas Canarias.* Santa Cruz de Tenerife, 1848. New edition with notes by Miguel de Santiago. Madrid. 1948-1960.

Ceballos L. and Ortuño F.: *Vegetación y Flora Forestal de las Islas Canarias Occidentales.* Instituto Forestal de Investigaciones y Experiencias. Madrid, 1951.

Espinosa, Fray Alonso de: *Historia de Nuestra Señora de la Candelaria.* Goya ed. Santa Cruz de Tenerife, 1952.

Fernández Navarro, Lucas: *Erupción Volcánica del Chinyero (Tenerife).* Anales de la junta de Ampliación de Estudios. Madrid, 1911.

Gaudio, Atilio: *Sur l'Origine des Canarians phehispanique.* Anuario de Estudios Mediterráneos, N. 4, Madrid-Las Palmas, 1958.

Hooton, Ernest A.: *The Ancient Inhabitants of the Canary Islands.* Harvard University-Cambridge, 1925.

Hörbiger, Fauth: *Glazial Cosmogonie.* Leipzig 1925.

Lajard, José: *Le Langage Sifflé des Canaries.* Journal of the Paris Anthropological Society, Paris, 1891.

Martel Sangil, Manuel: *Las Islas Canarias y su Origen.* Bilbao, 1950.

Millares Torres, Agustín: *Historia General de las Islas Canarias.* Las Palmas, 1893.

Rosa Olivera, Leopoldo, and Serra Rafols, Elías: *El Adelantado D. Alonso de Lugo y su Residencia por Lope de Sosa.* Fontes Rerum Canarium, III, Instituto de Estudios Canarios. La Laguna, 1952.

Rumeu de Armas, Antonio: *El Obispado de Telde.* Madrid, 1960.

Saurat, Denis: *La Atlántida. Historia y Leyenda.* Foreword by Rafael Ballester Escalas. Translation and Appendices by José Castellano. Barcelona-Mateu (undated).

Torriani, Leonardo: *Descripción e Historia al Reino de las Islas Canarias.* Translated from the Italian with notes by Alejandro Cioranescu. Santa Cruz de Tenerife, 1959.

Verneau, Dr. R.: *Cinq Annés de Sejour aux Yles Canaries.* Paris, 1891.

Viera y Clavijo, José de: *Noticias de la Historia General de las Islas Canarias.* Vols. I, II and III. Goya ed. Santa Cruz de Tenerife, 1950.

Wirth, Hermann: *Der Aufgang der Menschheit,* Jana, 1929.
— *Die Heilige Urschheit,* Leipzig, 1931.

OTHER BOOKS BY PROFESSOR HERRERA ABOUT TO BE ISSUED

— *La Atlántida de Platón, un Continente de elevada civilización antes del Diluvio.*

— *Un español universal: José de Anchieta en la Historia del Brasil.*